A JOHN CATT PUBLICATION

T0266145

AN EDUCATOR'S GUIDE TO
MENTAL HEALTH AND WELLBEING IN SCHOOLS

JAMES HOLLINSLEY

First Published 2018

by John Catt Educational Ltd,
12 Deben Mill Business Centre, Old Maltings Approach,
Melton, Woodbridge IP12 1BL

Tel: +44 (0) 1394 389850 Fax: +44 (0) 1394 386893
Email: enquiries@johncatt.com
Website: www.johncatt.com

ISBN: 978 1 911382 62 1

Set and designed by John Catt Educational Limited

CONTENTS

Disclaimer

The aim of this book is to tell our experiences with honesty. Consequently, some chapters may trigger an adverse reaction. If a chapter is beginning to upset you, we advise that you immediately please stop reading and seek help or support. We are not doctors, therapists or experts on mental health conditions and disorders.

About the contributors

Roy Blatchford CBE

Dr. Roy Blatchford is the Executive Director of Education in the Office of the First Deputy Prime Minister of the Kingdom of Bahrain.

From 2006-2016 he was Director of the National Education Trust in the UK – an independent foundation that leads excellent practice and innovation in education. Previously he served as one of Her Majesty's Inspector of Schools (HMI) in England, with national responsibilities for school improvement and for the inspection of outstanding schools. Roy has extensive experience of writing inspection frameworks, nationally and internationally, and has inspected and reviewed over 1000 schools and colleges in Europe, USA, Middle East and India.

For 30 years, Roy has been an international trainer and speaker on English and literacy, school improvement, leadership and innovation. He has served as an adviser to various UK governments, including Deputy Chair of the DfE Teachers' Standards Review (2012) and of the Headteachers' Standards Review (2014). Roy is a Visiting Fellow at Oxford Brookes University and is co-founder of the Mumbai-based education foundation Adhyayan. He is the author/editor of over 150 books. He was awarded Commander of the Most Excellent Order of the British Empire (CBE) for services to education in the 2016 New Year Honours.

James Hollinsley

James Hollinsley is the headteacher of a two-form primary academy that has received both regional and national awards for mental health and wellbeing. He is a qualified Special Educational Needs Coordinator (SENCO), holds the national qualification for School Inspectors (NPQSI) and an MA in Specific Learning Difficulties and Special Educational Needs. James has written pieces and collaborated with groups such as YoungMinds and Education Policy Institute (EPI) to develop ideas for campaign strategy and best practice in schools. He was previously Lead Professional for Special Educational Needs and Disability (SEND) in a London borough and is also a school governor. He has 20 years' experience in teaching and leadership in both mainstream primary and special secondary sectors. Longwood Primary Academy, formally in Special Measures, was graded as Good with Outstanding leadership and management, along with Personal Development, Behaviour and Welfare, in less than three years of opening.

head@longwood.netacademies.net

@hollinsley

Lewis Terry (Illustrations)

Lewis Dexter Terry is an artist and a teacher, living and working in Essex. Lewis has exhibited his art nationally in galleries and at popular London-based conventions. He has also worked on various commissions for both public and private clients.

Lewis continues to work in the teaching profession, applying his creative gifts to inspire and stimulate the classroom. He also continues to illustrate and paint, as well as regularly documenting his artistic exploits.

Hannah Ewers

Hannah Ewers is Deputy Headteacher at Longwood Primary Academy, Harlow. She is a qualified SENCO and is Head of Longwood's Outreach Team for Mental Health, Behaviour and Wellbeing. Hannah is part of a leadership team, recently graded by Ofsted as Outstanding, that seek to enhance and support better wellbeing and mental health through school to school support and speaking at regional training events. Her 2009 study into 'Disney characters and the effect on children's body-image' is currently part of a wider collection of research into this issue.

Gillian Kierans

Gillian Kierans was Headteacher of Aultmore Park Primary School and LCR (Language Communication Resource). Previously, Gillian was director at Glasgow East Women's Aid. She was also a finalist as Headteacher in the national Place2Be awards in 2016.

James Kenyon

James has worked in primary schools for 21 years. He spent seven years as the Deputy Headteacher of Hillyfield Primary School, a large outstanding primary school in Walthamstow. James is now the Headteacher of Chapel End Junior Academy and part of the REAch2 Academy Trust. Previously in Special Measures, Ofsted recently recognised the school as a good school with outstanding leadership and behaviour and safety. James also works as a Leadership Partner for REAch2 and has supported three other schools in their improvement. James is a governor of the Harlow Cluster of schools within NET. He has a six-year-old adopted son.

Jamesmk1974@gmail.com

Jennie Giovanelli

Jennie Giovanelli is Headteacher at Kingsthorpe College, a Leading Edge school. Previously Vice Principal at an outstanding school with responsibility for leading learning and teaching, and standards and achievement. Regardless of strategic area of responsibility, Jennie is passionate and committed to developing a culture that recognises the importance of both staff and student wellbeing through ensuring the development of leadership behaviours, and making sure operations, strategy, and culture are aligned.

Jennie has presented at several national conferences and tweets/blogs under @beautifullyfra1.

Jon Reid

Jon Reid (MSc Oxon, PCTHE, PGDES, PGCE, BA Hons, MBPsS, FHEA) joined Oxford Brookes University as Senior Lecturer in SEN/Inclusion following a teaching career in both primary and secondary education. During his mainstream educational experiences, Jon developed an interest in supporting pupils with additional learning needs. Subsequently, he spent time teaching in a therapeutic residential school catering for pupils who had experienced severe emotional trauma due to the accumulation of adverse experiences in infancy and early childhood. He later became the Deputy Headteacher of an Independent Secondary SEMH School that specialised in supporting pupils with complex educational needs, communication difficulties and challenging behaviours.

j.reid@brookes.ac.uk

Marc Rowland

Head of the Research School based at Rosendale Primary School Former Director of Policy and Research for the National Education Trust from 2007 to 2017. Over the past four years, Marc has worked with Rosendale on two major school-based research projects on Lesson Study and Metacognition. The second edition of his book *An Updated Practical Guide to the Pupil Premium* was published in December 2015 (John Catt Educational). John Catt Educational also published his latest book, *Learning without Labels*, in March 2017. Marc is currently working with the Jersey government on the introduction of a 'Jersey Pupil Premium' and with Learn Sheffield on their Priorities Project. He is also the co-author of the Essex LA-funded Pupil Premium self-evaluation toolkit and has worked with North Yorkshire, Essex, Sheffield, Hampson, Swindon and Warwickshire LAs on year-long projects to support better outcomes for disadvantaged pupils. Marc has worked with over 300 schools to support them with their strategy to improve outcomes for disadvantaged pupils, and spoken to approximately 6000 school leaders in conferences on Pupil Premium, from Northumberland to Cornwall.

marcrowland@rosendale.cc

Manisha Tailor MBE

Manisha Tailor MBE is the founder of Swaggarlicious who uses the power of football and education to engage with diverse community groups and organisations, including women and girls and adults with mental illness to lead a healthy lifestyle and develop life-long learning skills. By profession Manisha is a qualified headteacher, primary school trained with a Masters degree, and more than 15 years of experience working in schools across the UK and Internationally. She is also only one of 19 Asian women (based on FA historical data over 20 years) to hold the prestigious UEFA B Licence in Football Coaching.

Dr Zenovia Christoforu

Zenovia Christoforu is a Clinical Psychologist specialising in working with children and adolescents with mental health difficulties.

Dr Sapphire Weerakone

Sapphire Weerakone is a Clinical Psychologist specialising in working with individuals with a diagnosis of Personality Disorder.

Kate Armstrong-Taylor

Kate Armstrong-Taylor (MA, MSc, PGDip) is a specialist counsellor working with children and young people in schools. She also works for the leading children's mental health charity, Place2Be. Her interest in mental health and early intervention began with her studies at the Anna Freud National Centre for

Children and Families and she is passionate about the promotion of wellbeing for all in the school environment.

Tom Rogers

Tom Rogers is a Head of History and Founder of TMHistoryIcons (the national Teachmeet for history teachers). He is a weekly columnist for the *TES* (Times Educational Supplement). He has over ten years worth of classroom experience and is course curator for Udemy. You can also find Tom at rogerhistory.com.

@RogersHistory

Pran Patel

Assistant Principal Curriculum and Standards at the Mark Hall Academy in Harlow, Essex. BSc Hons in Physics at the University of Birmingham. QTS through a GTRP from the University of Wolverhampton. NPQSL from future leaders on whole-school coaching. Teaching for 13 years in East Africa, London and the West Midlands.

@MrPatelsAwesome

A huge thanks also to the brave voices from school professionals who have shared their experiences, although some are understandably anonymous.

To Nic, Brax and Matt.

To my magical reason for being (a very big part of my very small world).

Promise me you'll always remember:

'You're braver than you believe, stronger than you seem, and smarter than you think.' – A.A Milne

FOREWORD BY ROY BLATCHFORD CBE

I started teaching in Her Majesty's Prison, Brixton in 1973. When I moved to teach in a south London primary school I vowed that all my 'top juniors' would leave me with strong self-esteem and the dignity of articulacy and literacy, as prerequisites for success at secondary school.

'Mental health' was not in my vocabulary as a young teacher. However, it is rightly in the minds of students, parents and teachers today. My experience in schools over four decades tells me that children and young people cannot flourish in the school environment unless their self-esteem and readiness to learn are carefully nurtured by skilled teachers and support staff.

Two years ago I had the privilege to be a member of the Education Policy Institute's Commission, which produced the influential report 'Children and Young People's Mental Health: Time to Deliver'.[1]

In that role I saw first-hand the wide variance of practice within NHS services for those children and young people with mental health issues. I came to understand the imperative that we share nationally the very best local practices. I also came across the excellent work of James Hollinsley (editor of this collection) at Longwood Primary Academy, Harlow.

At the launch of the EPI report, Secretary of State Jeremy Hunt spoke eloquently and personally about the issue of online bullying, and how, as a parent of three young children, he was keenly aware of what some parents and teachers have to manage. Hunt observed that when he was a child, if you were bullied at school at least you could escape when you went home. But pernicious texting means a young person today finds it difficult to escape.

The delivery of effective services clearly hinges upon the many NHS partners involved. Yet it is teachers that are de facto in the frontline when it comes to children's emotional wellbeing. Hence the need for mental health training to be part of initial and in-service provision for teachers.

Further, we need to see a trained lead for mental health and wellbeing in every school and ensure that young people are involved in designing in-school

---

1   Frith, E. (2016): Children and Young People's Mental Health: Time to Deliver. London: Education Policy Institute.

support. Personal and social education programmes require a particular focus on the risks of contemporary social media and how pupils can build their resilience to confront its worst aspects.

What gives me particular optimism is that we shall increasingly succeed in early identification and successful treatment of mental ill health in the young is the willingness of adults from all backgrounds to talk about the issue. As recently as five years ago, this was not the case.

The subject is properly on the national agenda, politically and socially. This collection of essays is happy evidence of that much-needed coming together of professionals from different backgrounds, speaking powerfully about their important work with children and young people and their own personal experiences.

... RIGHT?

I wake up every day wondering what if I said the truth about me, about how I feel? Stopped living a lie. You see, the longer I do, the harder it gets. Every moment is a struggle to seem normal; to smile, to mask up and to put up.

But I am a normal human being... right?

Those voices, ever growing in the media population resonate through my soul 'it's okay, break the stigma'. But what would they make of me? Like unwanted truths in a relationship that are there but never told, I say nothing in fear that it might break what I have left. I look in the mirror but don't recognise the person that others see.

But I'm a normal parent... right?

I wipe away the tears before school, and later after INSET. I would drink my soul away given half a chance. But my responsibility, my life, calls for order. So I cling on to what is reality, part hoping to conceal, part wanting to be caught so I can say 'I'm not okay'; my finger constantly on the self-destruct button.

But I'm a normal teacher... right?

I look to religion, to music, to walks in the country. I look to normality, to movies, to evenings out. I look to counselling, to friends, to loved ones. I look to social media, to food, to another. I turn to myself and ask 'why can you not just say it to someone?'.

The bell goes again...

Children walk into class...

And I wonder...

You will be okay... right?

But how many of you will feel like me? How many of you are stronger-willed? How many of you less resilient or without a foundation to survive? How many of you will suffer, even though you are 'academically successful'?

Then I realise... something needs to change... there needs to be a greater voice... right?

The same thing shouldn't happen to our next generation. Change is needed. The politics, the targets, the aspirations, the accountability procedures, the frameworks, goals and ethos – all need re-definition.

Because I am a normal human being, parent and teacher and it's the time to change. It is time to speak up and, more importantly, act.

The question is not 'am I normal?'. The question is this: 'do you hold an educated voice of reason *or* do you have a voice in need of being reasonably educated?'

When it comes down to mental health and wellbeing within schools and beyond, there is much education to do.

Poor mental health lies dormant and potentially in every human, regardless of status – some are just luckier than others without it waking up. To ensure that our actions truly matter our children need us, the profession, to change the agenda.

It is time for wellbeing to rise alongside grades and be given the same gravitas as academic outcomes. Only then will the difference we make have true meaning.

You agree with that... right?

You are going to help make a change... right?

You see the implications of what could be if we don't... right?

... right?

– Thomas Campbell, primary school teacher and survivor of poor mental health.

'Once the understanding is there, we can all stand up and not be ashamed of ourselves, then it makes the rest of the population realise that we are just like them but with something extra.' – Stephen Fry

CHAPTER 1
The importance of mental health in schools

A quick note to the reader... I have rewritten this a dozen times over – some more emotive and some less, some fact-based and some anecdotal. I came to the conclusion that no matter what I write, it cannot emphasise enough the importance of wellbeing in schools – especially for those institutions and organisations with an infatuation of academic outcomes. These outcomes will mean very little without the contents of this book, and for some vice versa. I think the quote below is a good starting point, so let's go with that.

'A child's mental health is just as important as their physical health and deserves the same quality of support. No one would feel embarrassed about seeking help for a child if they broke their arm – and we really should be equally ready to support a child coping with emotional difficulties.' – HRH Duchess of Cambridge

This sums up, perfectly, the current status of Britain's mental health. As a society we have sat on a quiet, ever delicate, three-legged stool. On top of which is a child who, with an incessant need to rock backwards, is just waiting to fall.

The reason that people like you or I went into the world of education is to make a difference, and we do. Yet within the educational system itself, there is a top-heavy focus on attainment, progress and outcome measures. This may be understandable, given the pressures of an ever-shrinking world and global workplace that our children will have to contend in later life. It is easily reasoned, measurable, and important, until you understand the larger, widespread problem surrounding mental health in schools and beyond.

And herein lies the problem

Not being a lover of statistics, I loathed putting any in. It seems to somewhat undermine the suffering that is taking place. Yet, without it a clear picture of our national predicament cannot be seen.

- In early 2016 a snapshot survey by the NAHT of 1455 headteachers in England suggested that two-thirds of primary schools are not equipped to support mental health concerns.
- In 2016, and then again in 2017, Ofsted released that 90% of primary schools were rated Good or Outstanding.

The evidential gap between standard of school and ability to cope with mental health concerns highlights how the mental wellbeing of pupils is not necessarily high within current educational accountability processes. As such, the mental health of this nation is at constant risk. Without placing a wider emphasis on, and support for schools; depression, anxiety, suicide rates, amongst many other mental health needs, will continue to rise and the effects will further regress our nation.

What will happen to the three quarters of a million?

Mental health is responsible for an increasing epidemic of harm to our youngest members of society. The damage in later life can be life-limiting, life-threatening, irreparable and lead to further generations experiencing the same. For those that are lucky, help is found. For those that are less lucky, they suffer. For those unfortunate, the consequences are incomprehensible.

- 10% of children and young people (aged 5-16 years) have a clinically diagnosable mental health problem, yet 70% of these have not had appropriate interventions at an early age.[2]
- 1 in 12 young people self-harm at some point in their lives, though there is evidence that this could be a lot higher. Girls are more likely to self-harm than boys.[3]

2   Children's Society. (2008): The Good Childhood Inquiry: health research evidence. London: Children's Society.
3   Brooks, F. (2015): HBSC England National Report 2014. Hatfield, UK: University of Hertfordshire.

- Suicide is the leading cause of death in young people (male and female) in their 20s and early 30s. Hanging preferred by males, poisoning by females. Suicide attempts are up to 20 times more frequent than completed suicides.[4]

- 95% of imprisoned young offenders have a mental health disorder. Many of them are struggling with more than one disorder.[5]

- Along with the detrimental price to the individual and their families, the long-term cost to the UK economy is £105 billion per year.[6] This is in reaction to what is already being caused.

MENTAL HEALTH IN BRITISH SCHOOLS

11,706,675

Children and Young People in education (aged 3-18)

1,170,668

Children with mental health problems (1 in 10)

772,640

Children with mental health problems in unequipped schools

Based on average annual birth rate (2004-2014) of 780,445

The above does not take into account those that are yet to show signs and symptoms or the ever-increasing migrant trend. Only last week, I had a young boy join us, separated from his family, who walked to the UK from Afghanistan; his story was unimaginable, but his needs were no less.

The UK is currently looking at over 772,000 individuals with mental health problems of whom schools feel that they are not equipped to provide support for. 772,000 is a number greater than the entire population of Leeds or 61 times the full capacity of Wembley Arena.

---

4   National Office of Statistics. (December 2017). Statistical bulletin: Suicides in the UK: 2016 registrations. London: National Office of Statistics.

5   YoungMinds. (2014): Same Old... the experiences of young offenders with mental health needs. London: YoungMinds.

6   Department of Health. (2016): No health without mental health: A cross-Government mental health outcomes strategy for people of all ages Supporting document – The economic case for improving efficiency and quality in mental health. London: Department of Health.

The darkness...

The following assertions can be made regarding the current status of our education system:

- The pressures on schools is unforgiving – for outcomes, not happiness or feeling whole.

- Schools are in need of further training on developing good mental health and access to better services (as stated before two-thirds of heads are leading schools that are 'not equipped').

- Referrals to Child and Adolescent Mental Health Services (CAMHS) or Emotional Wellbeing and Mental Health Service (EWHMS) are inundated – requests made by schools are either lower than the threshold or have waiting times. It was uncovered in 2016 that the median of the maximum waiting times for all providers was 26 weeks for a first appointment and nearly ten months for the start of treatment.[7]

- Therefore, schools need to provide further support and care for those vulnerable with mental health needs that they are unsure of, diagnosed or not, to fill the void and ever-growing need for underfunded public sector systems (as only 0.7% of current national expenditure is on mental health).[8]

- Without a greater emphasis on ensuring that the children are mentally well and resilient, life outcomes will not improve.

- If schools do not meet the needs of individuals with mental health problems, regardless of the increasing academic outcomes at school, these issues may well manifest and effect later life.

- The effects of which will have emotional impact on the next generation, which according to current trends, is still growing in number.

- Go back to the start of this list, just add on another 100,000 innocents or so.

... and the trailblazers

Yet there are solutions. This book is about caring for the most vulnerable in our society and shaping futures – sharing best practice in education and beyond. The light, shining without excuse and without fear, to lead towards further understanding and better outcomes for the whole person. The trailblazers for children's mental health:

---

7   Frith, E. (2016): CentreForum Commission on Children and Young People's Mental Health: State of the Nation. London: CentreForum.

8   Independent Mental Health Taskforce to the NHS. (2016): The Five Year Forward View for Mental Health. London: the Mental Health Taskforce (NHS).

- **School leaders and schools** that put every child first and recognise that the mental health and wellbeing of children is as high as, if not higher than, academic achievement.

- **Charities and think tanks** that put their Heads Together to increase strength in voice and an understanding of the wider mental health picture.

- **Brave and strong individuals** who have survived experiences with mental health who, in sharing, increase the understanding that at times 'it is ok not to be ok'.

Nelson Mandela once said that 'Education is the most powerful weapon you can use to change the world'. He is right, but education in Britain needs to be redefined to meet the needs of the human condition – rather than conditions set by others.

'There is no health without mental health.' – Dr. David Satcher

CHAPTER 2
We all have 'mental health' – it's what you do with it that counts

Within the media, there is a growing awareness and publication around 'mental health'. Over the years the terminology has changed and, more recently, so has perspective. As such, it is important to understand the link between history and present when looking at mental health.

A very, very brief history and why it is important
For the larger part of history, those with poor mental health were treated very poorly. In medieval times, it was linked to witchcraft and demons – mostly leading to attempted exorcism or burning at the stake. The scientific approach was through the drilling into the skull (trephining) to release the spirit. Before these times of 'medical' practice, it was linked to making gods angry.

The 1600s saw the growing introduction of lunatic asylums e.g. Bedlam, that saw the vulnerable removed from communities and kept in dismal, prison-like conditions including shackles and beating – seemingly a refuge for them with a focus on keeping them in. The 1800s started to see treatments such as rotation therapy in which a chair was suspended and the patient was spun in a circular motion until they promised the staff that they would get better. Over time these changed from being places in which those less affluent could be watched by visiting public to being redefined by the early 20th century as 'mental hospitals' with a more medical approach – the most common being electroconvulsive therapy and lobotomies being brought in within the 1930s until popular banning in the '50s.

In the 1970s many of the asylums or mental hospitals closed in growing favour of therapy, converting to what is now commonly known as short stay hospital placements – this was aided by the development and popularity of anti-psychotic medication and further understanding of therapeutic support. In both the UK and US, the percentage institutionalised decreased in 40 years by 90%, between 1950 and 1990. However, we are still in an age in which some generations of society experienced the large stigma of asylums and institutions – many of those most affluent would pay for these services in secret. Those who could not afford private placements would make up stories of holidays and visiting family. No wonder there is such mystery and stigma, only now beginning to be challenged – this will take anything from a decade onwards to educate society and convince communities and employers that it is okay to have a mental health condition.

We have a very long way to go. Last week, I spoke to a lady from Africa who hides her epilepsy from her family because they believe she is possessed. It has cost her a marriage and her children. Her medication is hidden from her family in fear of further isolation. In turn, this has brought on depression and anxiety. If a very common medical issue such as epilepsy is still misunderstood within some British communities, then a person with a mental health condition that is even less understood – such as bipolar, psychosis or schizophrenia – will certainly face a tougher challenge to feel complete within society, hold employment or a successful relationship.

Schools

In schools, teachers, support staff and school leaders all have their own experiences of children with a wide range of issues that they can recall – usually stemming around 'behavioural difficulties'. The prevalence of mental health in social media states astronomical situations. You will see statistical headlines such as:

- The Mental Health Foundation (2003) stated that over '450 million people worldwide have a mental health problem'.
- Time to Change stated that '1 in 4 people will have a mental health problem this year, but too many people are made to feel isolated and ashamed as a result'.

With 'mental health problems' being so apparently prevalent, it can be clearly stated that having poor mental health is all part of the human condition at some point in many people's lives and, due to its commonality in humans, should have no stigma attached. It is an unfortunate but perfectly natural thing to happen to any person at any point in one's life. As Harris (2017) states: 'If we stop assuming that good mental health throughout a lifetime is the norm, we can get a much sharper idea of why those who are fortunate with their mental health are able to stay well.'

Teachers would benefit therefore from taking a child and looking at whether they show signs of good mental health. This is detailed by Gunnar (2017), at the Institute of Child Development:

- They are curious and interested in the world.
- They are willing and wanting to learn.
- They can sit and reflect at times about what is going on.
- They have the ability to experience love, affection and emotions.
- They get upset when things are upsetting them and bring themselves back to a level state without needing intense intervention.

Nature and nurture

Mental health impairments can develop in early childhood. Shonkoff (2010) stated that it is scientifically proven that 'at a molecular level, ALL aspects of brain function are the result of interaction between genetics and experience'. As such, it is our genes, together with experiences, that set up the operating systems in our brains.

The Center on the Developing Child at Harvard University refers to three kinds of responses to stress. This is very clear for practitioners and can aid school professionals to understand the workings of the brain.

Stress response system	Examples of situations	Effects
Positive stress Positive stress response is characterized by brief increases in heart rate and mild elevations in hormone levels.	☐ First day with a new caregiver ☐ Receiving an injected immunisation	Positive stress response is a normal and essential part of healthy development.
Tolerable stress Tolerable stress response activates the body's alert systems to a greater degree as a result of more severe, longer-lasting difficulties.	☐ The loss of a loved one ☐ A natural disaster ☐ A frightening injury	If the activation is time-limited and buffered by relationships with adults who help the child adapt, the brain and other organs recover from what might otherwise be damaging effects.

Toxic stress		Without reducing instability quickly
Toxic stress response can occur when a child experiences strong, frequent, and/or prolonged adversity.	☐ Physical or emotional abuse ☐ Chronic neglect ☐ Caregiver substance abuse ☐ Caregiver mental illness ☐ Exposure to violence ☐ The accumulated burdens of family economic hardship ...without adequate adult support.	and effectively through the correct support, the above situations can weaken developing brain architecture and cause 'early adversity' in which the body's stress response system is permanently set on high alert. This can have lifelong effects on the person's physical and mental health.

How should schools perceive 'mental health'?

It is easy for schools to get lost in the whole 'do they or don't they have poor mental health' debate. Instead, it would be easier for schools to develop a 'mindset' that there are three types of poor mental health. The reason we should do this is because schools can potentially tackle poor wellbeing, whereas 'mental health problems' and 'major psychological disorders' they certainly cannot and need specialist support. You can split 'mental health' into a three main subsets – please note that the extensive list of mental health conditions is far larger – however, these tend to be the most prevalent in schools and provide a firm example for discussion:

Type	Condition	Initial response
Major psychological disorders There is suggested evidence that these are traceable to the same genetic variations.	Autism – early* ADHD – early* Clinical depression – late Bipolar disorder – late Schizophrenia – late	*Autism and ADHD are more commonly diagnosed in the primary years and have a heavier involvement with the SENCO, whereas those 'late' are more prevalent in secondary schools and in need of clinical help.
Mental health problems Needing referral More likely to be a result of environmental factors**	Post-Traumatic Stress Disorder Eating disorders Anxiety Depression Obsessive Compulsive Disorder Paranoia Self-harm Suicidal thoughts/tendencies	Referral to Lead for Wellbeing who should refer this to EWMHS – previously known as CAMHS.
Wellbeing Actions and states of wellbeing as a result of events	Loneliness Panic attacks Low self-esteem Stress Anger	Also referral to Lead for Wellbeing – wraparound meetings with parents and other professionals. These can be tackled within the school environment with professional advice where needed.

Nationally, those needing 'clinical' support (referral to EWMHS, doctors, clinical psychologists) are those not being able to access quick support, and are

23

occasionally rejected for support due to not 'meeting thresholds'. This debate aside, schools are placed in ever increasing circumstances in which they have to provide support within their own establishment. Onsite bought in counselling services (later discussed in this book) are growing to become a more popular solution.

Teachers are there to teach…
The primary role of a teacher is to educate and deliver lessons. In many ways, an effective teacher will ensure that the pastoral care and emotional wellbeing of a pupil in their care is also high on their agenda – that is why so many schools are good and so many children and young people feel safe at school. The question is not regarding the role of the teacher (as this is to teach, role model and care for those in their school), rather about the role of a school itself. Teachers and schools are not mental health specialists and must stay clear of diagnosing or trying to solve mental health problems. Schools also vary widely in regards to ethos, focus and expectation of pupils and staff.

A successful school develops an ethos and structures that encompasses a proactive development of the whole child. Some primaries look after pupils very well, but do not necessarily look at what is needed to make them well rounded or are often stretched to cope with academic pressures. It is, therefore, of utmost importance that the ethos of a school focuses around the development of the whole child with a purposeful focus on development of academics and, equal to this, wellbeing for later life.

It is not just the children
Staff can also find themselves in a situation in which they have poor mental health – this is increasingly prevalent as more practitioners find the courage to actively speak out. It is also important for teachers and school leaders to be aware of what makes a school a successful and encompassing environment in which those struggling are supported and given the necessary help and understanding.

The creation of a positive working environment not only helps staff but filters down to the pupils. This must come from headteachers and governors to carefully consider the work-life balance and the culture of the school – those that do not, risk not only the wellbeing of staff but that also of children and young people. Adults who model positive working relationships and communication are essential in building a community that enhances and embraces positive wellbeing for all.

The first, large step

In short, embrace wellbeing, together with increasing resilience, as this will aid in developing positive mental health now and later in life. When it comes to immediate mental health problems – always seek the guidance from professionals. How schools do this will very much depend on their specific intake and need against financial ability and priorities.

A positive step for schools would be to look at individuals, question what they need in order to be well-rounded persons able to cope with what life will throw at them e.g. are they shy, withdrawn in group situations, in need of seeking too much attention, lacking in social circles, fearing failure, grossly overweight and so on. Plan how to provide individuals with the necessary experiences or tools and then execute these in the same gusto as many execute booster classes for academic development. Aim for successful individuals in all aspects and the common purpose will not only make a significant difference in future years, but also will have the buy-in and support from staff.

References

Center on the Developing Child at Harvard University. (2017): Toxic Stress. Available at: developingchild.harvard.edu/science/key-concepts/toxic-stress/ (Accessed 29 July 2017).

Gunnar, M. (2017): Center on the Developing Child. In Brief: Early Childhood Mental Health. Available at: developingchild.harvard.edu/resources/inbrief-early-childhood-mental-health (Accessed 20 June 2017).

Shakoff, J. (2010): Building a New Biodevelopmental Framework to Guide the Future of Early Childhood Policy in *Child Development*. Washington, D.C.: The Society for Research in Child Development, Inc. Vol. 81, no. 1, p. 357-367.

Time To Change (2018): Be in your mate's corner and change a life – men urged in new mental health campaign. London: Time to Change. Available at: www.time-to-change.org.uk/news/be-in-your-mates-corner (Accessed 1 January 2018).

WHO (2003): Investing in Mental Health. Geneva: The World Health Organisation.

'Doubt is to certainty as neurosis is to psychosis. The neurotic is in doubt and has fears about persons and things; the psychotic has convictions and makes claims about them. In short, the neurotic has problems, the psychotic has solutions.' – Thomas Szasz

CHAPTER 3
Chalkface Survivors: Living with psychosis

Former learning support assistant, Birmingham

As a child I was very ill. I contracted German measles at six months old and later formed epilepsy as a consequence of the illness. At the age of three I missed out on a nursery placement due to having multiple seizures on a daily basis. I went to school in Reception. By then the medication was working, which allowed me to attend school on a semi-regular basis.

During the primary years I missed out on many experiences you would now call 'character defining', which would have equipped me more for life ahead. By the time I arrived in secondary school the epilepsy had worsened to the extent that I was only at school for half of the time I was meant to be. When I was at school I was commonly very tired due to the medication and, as a result, I spent the first couple of years unable to fully concentrate or meet my full academic potential.

Arriving back at school after time away was always stressful. I remember talking to a friend who explained that she was 'stressed' when she came back from an illness, only to find someone else sitting in her seat and how she had to make friends with another group of people in class. This was a frequent occurrence for me and made it very difficult to secure friendships and blend in. I was never bullied as such, apart from the occasional comments and jibes from teachers, such as 'oh, so you're back are you' and 'nice to see you actually bothered turning up'. I had a small group of good friends who I would also see outside of school, so I was never isolated.

It was in Year 9 that the first blow came. The options available became more limited because of my performance and lack of attendance. Since I had missed so much of school, I found that the absences served as motivation and I was driven to do even better. However, the school never provided any extra work for the time when I was at home and, consequently, I fell behind my peers and two years later my GCSEs were not enough to get me access to the course I wanted. I do believe that if I had been provided with more work to do outside of school then I would have achieved the grades I needed to, and should have, reached. Doors of opportunity were closed and my options were narrowed. I was given help at times but not enough to catch up – I became quieter and shyer as the years went on.

Before leaving we had a meeting with the careers officer – I explained that I wanted to do an NVQ in business studies but I was told I would only be able to do office studies (business administration). So that is what I did – and I loved it – four days' work experience with one-day college per week.

At the same time, during the summer holidays, my parents separated and divorced. Not getting onto the course that I wanted and having parents separating was hard – even at the age of 16 you want your parents around you to give support and it was hard coping at college – I was determined however to succeed and studied hard. I kept in contact with my dad but he was too far away to really help so I stayed with my mother, who was illiterate, and could not help with any homework or applications. She did not know when parents' meetings were and couldn't support me in the studies – so I went to college and saw my way through, gaining my NVQ2. Once completing the course, I sought employment working in an office and was able to hold the post for a year until my epilepsy again got worse and became unstable. After this I was able to get another job, only to be let go after a month due to ill health.

When I went to the job centre I was told that I was 'too sick' to be given employment and therefore should apply for income support. I wanted to do volunteering but only to be told that the same rules applied. So, from the age of 18 to 22 I was mostly unemployed – begrudgingly so! I worked in between for a disability advice line and general office-based temp work. It was at this time that I started to work as an office temp in a school; I found myself really enjoying this and something I was good at.

Psychosis was a word that I was not even aware of at this time in my life. I met a nice guy and moved away a year later. We were really happy for a while, travelling and exploring the world to places such as Thailand and Australia – really living. After that I remained in stable employment for five years as a learning support assistant after being placed into a class, from the office, to fill in for someone – I never looked back. I found something I loved and was not only good at but also got a lot back in return from the children. However, after these five years, I started to miss my family and felt isolated after not making many friends in the area. My partner did not want to move and we separated – I relocated back home with my mum.

Shortly afterwards I found it hard to get employed, especially in a school – I did some office temping for a mental health service to earn a living, completed a coaching course and was training with St John's ambulance. It was all too much to cope with – the break up, gradual unemployment, trying to better myself with courses and social isolation due to a lack of social circle or relationships. I felt so overwhelmed that in the end I couldn't cope.

I used to stay up all night, my brain not shutting down or switching off. I started overthinking everything and thoughts flooded my head on a constant basis. I had enough. I reached out to someone I knew and told them I wanted to end my life. I had no resilience left; I think that schools need to develop children with this so that they can cope with later life. I am sure that if I had developed more of this I don't think what happened next would have occurred.

I sat in the hospital waiting for the support team – they asked me if I wanted to be sectioned of my own accord – I said 'no' and ended up back at home with a prescription of Risperidone (an antipsychotic medication) along with a homecare package. I did not think of myself as someone with poor mental health, just someone who had been overwhelmed and too stressed to continue with my current situation. My health was affected and I was under an endocrinologist for hormonal imbalances associated with the treatment.

After six months, I started to do voluntary work in schools – was deemed as no threat to anyone after an Occupational Health referral and took full time employment again. I then met a great man and after a year moved in with him. We started to talk about children and by now, near approaching 40, I felt that this was our time to have children. I went to see the doctor about coming off the medication – we did, although at the time the doctor was going to increase the dosage.

I had three months of feeling 'normal' and trying for a baby before the relationship broke down. Again I moved back to my mum's place and after another four months it suddenly struck me. The episode was unlike the first one. Back then it was a gradual increase of stress and not being able to cope. This time around, I felt that I was doing fine – I was already in employment and doing well. It was all a blur really – me walking, needing to clear my head, the next minute I was on a roundabout surrounded by five police officers and two meat wagons.

I didn't want them in my way and didn't want them interfering – I just needed to have time by myself. I wasn't, again, a danger to anyone else but they saw that I needed help and took me to the hospital – this time I was given no choice. I was placed under Section 2 (under the mental health act someone can be detained in hospital for an assessment and treatment of their mental disorder) and left in the care of a mental health hospital.

There I had time to rest – I was on one ward for a week before going to another that was more social, I kept myself busy playing cards, reading and walking. It was a strange experience but I was well looked after. When leaving, I was clear about what happened and I am now on a high dose of Olanzapine, an antipsychotic medication. It works and I will stay on this. It has been three months since it happened and I am set to restart my work on a phased return. I feel better and can now think clearly.

Writing this and reflecting on my life has made certain things clear about wellbeing and education:

- Nursery education is a key part of any child's life and should not be optional. It is a key cornerstone in a child's life and shapes them as learners and individuals.

- When pupils miss school, all schools should ensure that gaps in knowledge or skills are filled in either at home or through catch up sessions.

- If there are pupils that do miss school often, teachers should keep an eye on their social inclusion – are the pupils able to join in lessons and do they have social circles in the playground?

- Those with low self-esteem need additional support to raise this over time – this is key to later success in life.

- Be mindful about closing doors and limiting options at school – champion those where possible to reach for courses or subjects that could be achieved with support.

- Pupils that experience parents divorcing, at any age, will require support – preferably someone onsite to talk to.
- Those with illiterate parents should be provided with additional homework, coursework and administrative (e.g. college applications) support.
- A curriculum that builds character and resilience through a range of experiences is crucial.
- Having a mental health disorder does not define you as a person – it is something that can be treated – after this those with disorders can function and be part of society just as well as those without.

I wasn't born with a mental health disorder. If the above was provided to me, I may have been able to cope with my life's occurrences and it may have been very different. To champion those most vulnerable early on when they need it is to change the course of a life.

Since the writing of this chapter, Anastasia relapsed back into a psychotic state. She lost her job, and frequently missed taking medication. She isolated herself, removing the remaining friends who tried to help her and pushed family members away. She was being supported by the NHS home team, who saw her on a daily basis to give her medication at home, before being sectioned again under Section 3 of the Mental Health Act.

'Everything not saved will be lost.' – Nintendo Wii quit screen

CHAPTER 4
A mission for primary schools

If you walk into the majority of schools within the UK, you will find warm, caring staff that try their very best for children. At the end of 2016, over 90% of English schools were rated by Ofsted as 'good or better'. As part of that process, the quality of 'personal development, behaviour and welfare' in which an outstanding school ensures:

'Pupils can explain accurately and confidently how to keep themselves healthy. They make informed choices about healthy eating, fitness and their emotional and mental wellbeing. They have an age-appropriate understanding of healthy relationships and are confident in staying safe from abuse and exploitation.'

That should surely bode well for mental health? Well, not necessarily. There are a series of problems if schools strive to accomplish this, and this only, in order to tick a box or meet the benchmark.

Problems inside the box

Firstly, and the most problematic of these, is the catch-22 situation of measuring success in developing wellbeing. The current process is arguably not enough and there is little guidance as to what schools should do. If any regulatory body raises the bar on mental health and wellbeing, it would be likely to seek evidence and proof. The current climate is heavy on achievement (attainment and progress) – more so because there is data and therefore a tangible measurement of success. By increasing accountability in this area, some schools would feel compelled to measure the success of happiness, behaviour improvements and evidence of well-balanced pupils in order to prove the school's effectiveness. This is neither a good use of time for schools and teachers or good practice and should be avoided.

Another problem is that the criteria does not go far enough for the development of mental health and wellbeing. For a child to be able to make informed choices about health aspects suggests that they are already in tune with themselves – this is not necessarily, again, the most important aspect when deeming the quality wellbeing provision in a school.

In addition to compound this, there is little out there that defines what 'great' wellbeing and mental health provision looks like. Schools are under increasing pressure to provide services such as counselling that are not easily or readily available without cost on the NHS through the Emotional Wellbeing and Mental Health Service (EWMHS).

Poor mental health may not necessarily be on the rise – it is difficult to definitively say as our awareness of this has risen dramatically over the last decade. In 2015 there were over 1000 mentions of children's mental health in UK newspapers, in 2011, one tenth of this. Further awareness will inevitably lead to more diagnoses within society. The population of the UK is also growing – as a result the number of people with poor mental health is also likely to rise.

Finally, there is the issue around poor mental health itself. When looking at the statistics based on the survey on the prevalence of mental health (2004 – another statistical report is to be released in 2018), the number of children aged two to five already displaying mental health concerns is very similar to that of eight to 17-year-olds. As a result, schools are already required to meet the mental health needs of a vast number of pupils aged five or below.

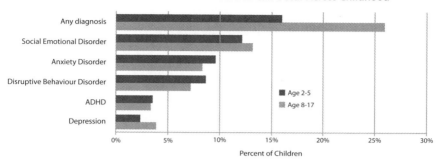

Mental Health Problems Can Occur Across Childhood

Source: Egger & Angold (2006)

The collective reason

When asking professionals from a range of schools to define, in one sentence, their reason for working in schools – the overwhelming consensus was defined as: 'to have productive, happy adults who are going to be part of successful communities'.

The key word within this is 'adults'. If primary – or indeed secondary – schools are to truly achieve what us as all professionals aspire to accomplish, then the nature of a school needs to change. By working backwards of what a successful adult is or could be, we can then define what we need to achieve as schools.

Developing happy, successful adults

There are a number of sources that would define 'happiness' and 'success'. The model, as you will see later, is not necessarily the most important aspect to consider, however it is the best starting point. Happy, successful adults are not made overnight – many issues relating to poor wellbeing in adults can relate back to childhood – thus the importance of developing the 'whole' person from an early age. In addition, by the nature of life, all people will have fluctuations in wellbeing and mental health over time with highs and lows, for example:

Highs: weddings, trips, events, success towards a goal, loving relationships, and friendships.

Lows: break down of relationships, bereavement for a loved one, poor health, job insecurity, financial difficulties, and stress at work.

It is important that schools aim to foster and develop children to be happy and successful adults. As adults, our sense of happiness is more complex than a child. There are a lot more life choices and aspects to juggle, such as work, looking after a family, bills, holidays, relationships and so on. For schools to start formulating or numerically accounting for pupils happiness or wellbeing is a slippery slope to further workload and nonsensical judgement of those we care for.

Nonetheless, schools can define what would best aid in developing well-balanced, thriving pupils. All of these aspects can be broken down into three key areas:

- Academic achievements
- Physical wellbeing
- Social and emotional security (Wellbeing and Mental Health)

If we, as schools, actively focus on raising the importance of academic/curricular success with that of wellbeing, and couple that with a focus on physical health, the outcomes and type of person moving on to their next step would be far more secure and ready for life than those who place grades/results as a definition of success.

Is this child eminently employable and happy?
It is a question I ask myself when children move on to secondary school. Are they well-rounded children, secure in themselves, socially robust, physically healthy and achieving as well as they can be? If so, great, if not, what could we have provided within our curriculum that would have led to a better outcome for this child? An ethos of no excuses with a surgical approach to developing individuals can make a very large difference. By asking key questions we can start to improve provision:

- Those who are reluctant to talk out aloud in class – how will you equip them with the skills and confidence to present to hundreds so that it does not hinder them in later life?

- Those who are lacking social skills – how will you develop this in everyday lessons so they have a good friendship group that will help them grow in character?
- Those who are in need to talking to a qualified professional? How will you ensure early access so that these issues are not carried into their later relationships?

There are so many questions that can be asked – by breaking down barriers to academic, social/emotional and physical development, schools can at least equip children at an early age with the knowledge and skills to cope with adversity. The barrier plan (described next and the 360 Approach Review in Chapter 22) does this well.

Providing the whole package – using barrier plans

It is important that schools prevent the possibilities of future poor mental health and wellbeing as much as possible. Many pupils in our care may experience challenges later in life. We will not be there to guide them but the experiences we give them now will shape their responses to these. To ascertain what pupils need, the initial creation and development of barrier plans can seem daunting and does take time. However, when complete, schools that have done these are in no doubt that the time used is beneficial.

The barrier plans

Section	Details
Interests Outside of school I am good at I need help with	It is important to ascertain the child's view of themselves. The 'interests' and 'outside of school' will provide a picture of their life outside of school. Do they take part in a range of activities, are their experiences limited? What are the hooks to engage those who are hard to reach? The other two sections 'I am good at' and 'I need help with' allows us to see the child' perspective of themselves – it may not necessarily be accurate but may show issues around self-esteem or an distorted view their learning.
Barriers	Be as honest and open as possible regarding these – list all aspects e.g. do they need glasses, lack a positive male role model, not have necessary resources at home, be reluctant to speak up in class, lack friendships…
My parents/carers feel	It is interesting to note, during informal talks or during parents evening the feelings around the parent/carer's feelings of how their child is doing as a whole person. Do they have any concerns or aspects with which they are positive?
Step to success	Combining the above, write a wish list for what the child or young person needs. For some this can be lengthy and comprehensive, for some possibly one or two points.

Suggested barrier plan format

It is important to note that the more honest and open the discussions regarding pupils and more detail that can be gathered the more effective they are. A suggested model for completing these is therefore a meeting (INSET or phase meetings) involving class teacher, support assistant, previous teacher (if close to beginning of academic year), SENCO where required, Family Support Worker, Safeguarding Lead and member of SLT. If not all can attend, the document can be updated and added to by the relevant parties. NOTE: as these are to be open and honest INTERNAL documents, a central secure storage of these is required – they are not necessarily to be shared with parents either – moreover a challenging reflection of what the pupil needs and what should be provided by the school to help the child and, at times, family.

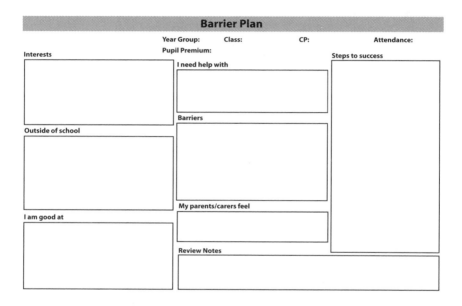

The mission is not to solve mental health problems, but to develop pupils to be well-balanced academically, physically and emotionally. Well-rounded people who have high quality experiences and belief in themselves are potentially more successful in later life. This will help reduce the potential of developing poor mental health or wellbeing when meeting challenges, thus making their education more meaningful. The proactive planning around this for individuals and catching the early warning signs is an essential part of reducing poor mental health in later society. You cannot foresee what will happen, but you can get them to a happier and more secure place within themselves.

References

Egger, H. L. & Angold, A. (2006) Common emotional and behavioural disorders in preschool children: Presentation, nosology and epidemiology. *Journal of Child Psychology and Psychiatry*, 47 (3-3), 313-337.

Office of National Statistics (2004): Mental health of children and young people in Great Britain. NHS. Available at: www.digital.nhs.uk/catalogue/PUB06116.

Ofsted (2018): Ofsted Inspection Handbook. Bristol: Ofsted.

'My advice is, never do tomorrow what you can do today.
Procrastination is the thief of time.' – Charles Dickens

CHAPTER 5
Best of British Practice

Hannah Ewers, Longwood Primary Academy

Research shows that across the UK, mental health issues in children are increasing while child wellbeing is deteriorating. Young people today have to navigate a complex and ever-changing world, facing challenges and pressures in numerous aspects of their life. Many children whose symptoms are spotted early may get the help they need, learning new skills to manage and cope and go on to live their life to its full potential.[9] As a school, we make it our priority to balance emotional wellbeing and academic learning, ensuring that measures are put in place to spot and intervene poor mental health at an early stage. This is what the whole school community wants from parents to teachers and, most importantly, it is what our children and young people deserve.

---

9   MQ: Transforming mental health. (2016): Young people's mental health. Available at: www. mqmentalhealth.org/articles/children-and-young-people

The facts

- 10% of children and young people (aged 5-16 years) have a clinically diagnosable mental problem, yet 70% of children and adolescents who experience mental health problems have not had appropriate interventions at a sufficiently early age.[10]

- 75% of those with a mental health condition start developing it before the age of 18.[11]

- Three children in every class have a diagnosable mental health condition.[12]

- Suicide is the most common cause of death for boys aged between 5 and 19, and the second most common for girls of that age.[13]

- Among teenagers, rates of depression and anxiety have increased by 70% in the past 25 years.[14]

- Mental health problems constitute the largest single source of world economic burden, with an estimated global cost of £1.6 trillion – greater than cardiovascular disease, chronic respiratory disease, cancer and diabetes on their own.[15]

- The Department for Education has found that, on average, children with higher levels of emotional, behavioural, social and school wellbeing, had higher levels of academic achievement and were more engaged in school.[16]

How do we promote emotional wellbeing in our school?

Most children attend school five days a week, where they spend over 7,800 hours throughout the course of their education. Schools are therefore well positioned to provide a model environment to promote good emotional wellbeing and identify early signs of poor mental health. For children experiencing difficulty

---

10 Mental Health Foundation (2017): Mental health statistics: children and young people. Available at: www.mentalhealth.org.uk/statistics/mental-health-statistics-children-and-young-people

11 Murphy, M and Fonargy, P. (2012): Mental health problems in children and young people In Annual Report of the Chief Medical Officer, Our Children Deserve Better: Prevention Pays. London: Department of Health and Social Care.

12 Green, H, Mcginnity, A, Meltzer, H, Ford, T, and Goodman, R. (2005): Mental Health of Children and Young People in Great Britain, 2004. Newport: Office for National Statistics.

13 Collishaw, S, Maughan, B, Goodman, R and Pickles, A. (2004): Time trends in adolescent mental health. *Journal of Child Psychology and Psychiatry.* Vol. 45, no. 8, p. 1350-1362.

14 YoungMinds (2017): Wise Up! Prioritising Wellbeing in Schools. Available at: youngminds. org.uk/media/1428/wise-up-prioritising-wellbeing-in-schools.pdf

15 Mental Health Foundation. (2015): Fundamental Facts about Mental Health. London: Mental Health foundation.

16 Gutman, L & Vorhaus, J. (2012): The Impact of Pupil Behaviour and Wellbeing on Educational Outcomes. London: Department for Education.

at home, school can also provide a consistent, safe and positive environment, offering a vital support network.[14]

Through different and varied approaches, as a school, we have created an environment to support children with poor mental health and equip teachers with the skills and knowledge to identify early signs of mental distress. We are already seeing the significant benefits of these approaches and are closer to achieving our vision of 'having productive, happy adults that are going to be part of thriving communities'.

Place2Be

Place2Be works with children in our school, offering them support to cope with emotional and behavioural difficulties. Children can access one-to-one counselling with a trained counsellor (short and long term), tailored to each child's needs. Teachers have seen this have a significant impact on the whole class and, through 'before and after' questionnaires, have reported on very positive changes in the children's behaviour and emotional wellbeing.

Children can also access Place2Talk, a drop-in/self-referral service open to all children. Pupils fill in a child-friendly slip (that can be accessed by all ages and abilities) outlining their problems and are allocated a trained adult to talk to. This gives children another outlet to discuss any issues they may have. Through Place2Talk, some children have been referred to one-to-one counselling after being identified as having poor mental health.

Place2Be have also provided group work on transition into secondary school and counselling and support services for parents and carers.

70 things at Longwood

Extracurricular activities promote social, emotional, physical and cognitive development. We have identified 70 activities that we believe all children should experience before leaving primary school. These activities range from sleeping under the stars, to hatching a chick, jumping over waves, to rock climbing. The activities have been carefully mapped out to ensure that in each academic year (from Reception to Year 6), children are experiencing a wide range of enriching activities. Due to the deprived backgrounds of our children, many of them are not exposed to these experiences outside of the school environment. It is a way to give them real experiences in the wider world and face a range of challenges that can significantly contribute to their personal development. We have seen it have a huge impact on children's self-confidence, self-esteem and resilience.

Art therapy

In our school, we have specialist teachers for English, maths, PE and art. Art has long been known to have therapeutic properties and a positive impact on mental health. Children can be inspired and motivated through engaging in art. It can also develop creativity and imagination, which can have a positive impact on other areas of the curriculum, as well as helping young people to develop the resilience to manage challenging life circumstances.[17] With this in mind, our art specialist teacher set up a long-term project, where children (some with poor mental health) would create an art piece. These sessions promoted resilience, teamwork and greatly improved self-confidence and self-esteem. The children reported a great sense of achievement at the end. Their work was showcased during an exhibition evening, which further promoted the feeling of success and triumph.

Mr or Little Miss Successful
Supporting children in identifying what it means to be a successful learner has been another priority of ours. It became apparent that, due to lack of positive role models, many children did not know what a successful learner looked like. Because of this, we developed the 'Mr or Little Miss Successful' initiative. Through adapting eight well-known Mr Men characters, to include characteristics of a success learner, children are now able to identify fundamental successful attributes. The characters include: Little Miss Self Confident, Little Miss Trustworthy, Little Miss Independent, Mr Appreciative, Mr Determined, Mr Kind, Mr Responsible and Little Miss Respectful. We have now recently introduced 'Mx Okay' – a character to promote self-acceptance, along with LGBT inclusion. We have an eye-catching display, outlining each of the characters along with examples of how to display each characteristic. Children use voting slips to nominate their peers for displaying these characteristics and an example of how they have done so. If a child gets nominated for every characteristic, they receive a reward badge.

The Daily Mile
A study of 10,000 primary school children across the UK found that two thirds of them lacked basic fitness.[18] According to The Daily Mile Foundation, its purpose is 'to improve the physical, emotional and social health and wellbeing of our children – regardless of age or personal circumstances'. Each day, in addition to break and lunch times, children and their teachers run a mile. The impact can be significant – improving not only children's fitness, but also their concentration levels, mood, behaviour and general wellbeing.

---

17   City Arts (2017): Art works: Using the arts to promote emotional health and wellbeing in schools. London: Speechmark Publishing Ltd. Available at: city-arts.org.uk/wp-content/uploads/2013/03/Art-Works.pdf

18   Thedailymile.co.uk (2018): About The Daily Mile. Available at: thedailymile.co.uk/about (Accessed: 1/1/2018).

Some of the other benefits to The Daily Mile include:

- Within four weeks, children who do The Daily Mile become fit.
- The 15-minute break from lessons is invigorating and leaves children more focused and ready to learn.
- The time spent outside, in all weathers, helps children become better engaged with the outdoors and aware of their surroundings.
- The Daily Mile is non-competitive, fully inclusive, and the children have fun!
- The Daily Mile is also a social occasion, and improves relationships, giving children the opportunity to talk to their peers and teachers in a way they might not in the classroom.
- The Daily Mile builds teamwork and leadership skills, with children helping and encouraging their peers.
- Children bring the benefits home, eating and sleeping better and encouraging their families to get active together.
- The Daily Mile builds self-esteem and confidence, improving children's perception of exercise for life.

The Kenny Approach
One of our pupils, Cerys Kenny, developed The Kenny Approach to help other pupils explore their feelings and feel safe. Cerys was awarded Place2Be Child Champion in 2016. As a result, our school has been generously awarded with funding to further develop materials for The Kenny Approach.

The Kenny Approach includes various booklets that encourage children to explore their feelings. This includes a scribble page, a place to write down feelings and instructions of how to breathe.

From this, we have created a wellbeing committee, made up of children from Year 5 and Year 6. Their role is to support children, in our wellbeing centre, during break and lunch times. They ensure that The Kenny Approach materials are available and can support children in filling out the booklets. They also offer children someone else to talk to, if they feel that they cannot talk to an adult. For the wellbeing committee, having such an important role in school, gives them a great sense of responsibility.

We will continue to promote emotional wellbeing and develop ways in which children can receive support and guidance. We believe it is our duty to provide children with the opportunity to succeed not only academically, but also emotionally, preparing them for the world beyond primary school.

'Every day, in a hundred small ways our children ask, 'Do you see me? Do you hear me? Do I matter? Their behaviour often reflects our response.' – L. R. Knost

CHAPTER 6
Setting an ethos: The PROGRESS approach

The Education Policy Institute's Young Mental Health Commission looked at how schools can adopt a whole school approach to prevention of mental health problems. One such school, Longwood Primary Academy in Harlow, has developed an approach called 'PROGRESS', which has led to improved outcomes for pupils that have social, emotional and mental health needs.

Provide a place to talk and feel protected

Raise the roof of resilience

Openly celebrate achievements

Grow and nurture the family unit

Rapid intervention and referral

E-safety to reduce risk

Strive to create a secure utopia

Stability and clarity in behaviour

Provide a place to talk and feel protected

- Use 'Time to Talk' with Place2Be. This is an additional service, outside of the 12 counselling sessions, and is an approach that can be used by all schools. Pupils fill in a form and put it in a post box. They can select an adult to talk to and name a friend they would like to join them.
- Really listen to pupils when they come to you – what may seem a trivial matter could appear colossal to them. Follow up with them – this way they know you care.
- Enhance pupil voice – Pupil Advocates, Class Advocates, School Improvement Officers, House Captains, School Council, voting stations, fortnightly votes and take on board their ideas for school events. Include those most vulnerable – develop their inner voice.
- Ensure whole staff awareness of those pupils who are vulnerable.

Raise the roof of resilience

- Know the limit of the most volatile pupils, and then raise it inch-by-inch over time. Know when to change focus and not continue to avoid failure.
- Allow the pupils to reflect when they are in a place to do so after an incident – what happened? What shall we do next time?
- Focus on the cause, not the behaviour – be calm in the face of outbursts – maintain a supportive relationship.
- Develop trust over time (including maintaining the behaviour policy) and keep consistent – for some this will take months, if not more.
- Develop an ethos of self-belief 'we cannot… yet', rather than 'we cannot.'

Openly celebrate achievements

- Some children want to be praised but do not like this in a large forum e.g. assemblies. A simple high-five and a smile can be just as powerful as being on stage. Showing work to a friend or significant adult works well for those not liking attention.
- Develop a cluster of well planned 'praise' routes – brilliant book, house points, reward time, headteacher awards, class points, emails/phone calls home, activities. These are to be within the behavioural approach and all adults are to be aware of these.
- Use art to increase the self-confidence and status of some vulnerable pupils (pieces commissioned onto acrylic) and include their work in an art exhibition to which families will be invited.

Grow and nurture the family unit

- Take time to know the parents and also the wider family e.g. it could be the older sibling who supports the parents in making important decisions.
- Presentations and workshops – engage those hard to reach families.
- Family Support Worker and Safeguarding Officer – both with an open all hours policy.
- Develop the parents' trust in the school, the headteacher and all staff – many parents have poor school experiences and believe this is still the case for their child. Knock down the barriers and let them see for themselves that things have changed.
- Focus on 'working together' – a two-way street rather than the school doing something to the family or individual. Communication is key.

Rapid intervention and referral

- Open dialogue regarding concerns as quickly as possible – try to grasp a picture of the reasons behind the concerns. Liaise with all adults, family and services where needed.
- Well placed interventions such as Lego therapy, emotional literacy for those that would benefit.
- Know when a child's needs require outside support and referral to CAMHS – do not risk their mental health getting worse by thinking it can be solved in-house or hoping it will go away over time.
- Accept that sometimes the answer is not within your school, but lies in your responsibility to find a placement promptly that matches the child and family situation.

E-safety: reducing bullying, grooming, radicalisation and abuse

- Ensure that pupils build resilience in staying safe and making safe decisions online.
- Educate parents about the risks associated with Facebook, Snapchat, Instagram, Kik, MySpace, Yik Yak, WhatsApp, Facebook Messenger, Skype... even gaming on the Xbox. These are diverse and open pupils to a range of threats. Educate adults in what to look for.
- Actively engage with families who allow young pupils to have phones.

Strive to create a secure utopia

- Zero clutter.
- Calming music in the corridors.

- An expectation of tranquil transitions in the building.
- Lockers for belongings – safe, tidy and secure.
- Adults modelling correct behaviour and communication between one another and to others.
- A sense of understanding and security to their needs – MDAs and LSAs trained to ensure smooth lunchtimes in which people 'listen'. One person not engaged within the school's approach can be significantly damaging.
- Carefully selected and commissioned artwork to raise self-esteem of vulnerable pupils.

Stability and clarity in behaviour
- Most importantly – have the children own the policy and know clear, consistent consequences for unwanted actions, but also routes for praise and reward – the clearer it is, the safer they feel.
- Proactively tackle bullying and issues around diversity, including guest speakers, lessons and assemblies. Communicate clearly to the school population actions taken for any possible occurrences.
- Explore the positive uses of phone/iPad technology to engage pupils and parents in sharing positive and negative learning behaviours.
- High communication and clarity levels to all.
- Ensure pupils are aware of individuals' triggers and develop a respect and understanding that we are all different but all deserve the same, such as respect, care, attention, understanding and emotional support.

'And those that were seen dancing were thought to be insane by those
who could not hear the music.' – Friedrich Nietzsche

CHAPTER 7
Musicality

There is something non-educational, something primal and soulful, about music. Most of us have songs or rhythms that we associate with different people, times, places and occasions. Some can make you smile, giggle, cry or feel melancholy. Some are private, some are shared and some can be made public to others.

I remember being with my eldest son when he was four months old. My wife went away for the weekend and I was left with all the usual bags, bottles and regimes in tow. On a dark Sunday evening, he started to cry and nothing would consul him. I tried everything I could think of for 90 minutes and was at my wits end. I turned on MTV for some music – a last-ditch attempt for support and a solution. More screaming succeeded, until 'Pumped up Kicks' by Foster the People came on. I had to play the track for 45 minutes straight, rewinding to the start with ear-piercing anger in between until he fell asleep. Admittedly, I am still not a fan of the song but, when I do hear it, I am taken back to something special, a bond. Within me there is calmness and a sense of belonging. Isn't it strange how we associate music with feelings?

Outside of the education spotlight and what can we learn

The same can be said for music generally changing the way people act and react. The first London tube station to play classical music was Elm Park on the District Line back in 2003. Train drivers were reported to be scared of stopping due to growing gang culture so they tried playing classical pieces – based on previous seemingly successful attempts in the 1990s in Canada – to disperse groups showing antisocial behaviour.

The result was that robberies were down by 33%, vandalism by 37% and assaults by 25%. There was also an overwhelming agreement from a survey of 700 passengers that 'hearing classical music made them feel happy, less stressed and relaxed'.

Top ten research pieces linking benefits of music to wellbeing and learning

Sing together more: Research (Eerola and Eerola, 2009) studied the social benefits in the school environment of 735 pupils in Finland, aged 9-12 across ten schools, before and after they were provided with extracurricular music classes. The results disclosed that extended music education enhances the quality of school life (QSL), particularly in areas related to general satisfaction about the school and a sense of achievement and opportunity for students. This was later followed-up by comparing to pupils attending other extended services, such as sports and visual arts – the results, again, highlighted that it was music that had the greatest benefit.

Music can affect your heart rate and stress levels: Research from Germany in 2009 by Trappe showed that music might have an effect on a person's heart rate. It also suggests that carefully selected music may be effective method to reduce anxiety and to improve quality of life, stating:

'The most benefit on health is visible in classic music, meditation music whereas heavy metal music or technosounds are even ineffective or dangerous and will lead to stress and/or life-threatening arrhythmias. There are many composers most effectively to improve QoL [quality of life], particularly Bach, Mozart and Italian composers are 'ideal'.'

It also claimed that relaxing music 'decreases significantly the level of anxiety in a preoperative setting to a greater extent than orally-administered midazolam' [anaesthesia and procedural sedative].

Music may reduce depression and helps you to sleep: In 2008, Harmat, Takacs and Bodizs researched nearly 100 students between 19 and 28 with sleep complaints. They listened to relaxing classical music at bedtime for 45 minutes every day for three weeks. The results showed that sleep quality has significantly improved along with a decrease in depressive symptoms. This is significant for people who suffer from depression as 90% of these also experience insomnia.

Listening to music may have a long-term effect on our mental health: In 2015, Carlson *et al* researched the neural activity of participants as they tuned in to happy, sad or fearful sounding music. Responses were assessed on several markers of mental health including depression, anxiety and neuroticism.

The findings showed that 'the possibility that an individual's use of music, particularly in response to negative affect, may relate to his or her mental health, as evidenced by correlations between listening tendencies as mental health outcomes'.

It also highlighted that 'diversion' (in using music to distract from negative thoughts) and solace (listening to negative music reflecting the listener's mood but providing comfort) was more beneficial, particularly for women, than 'discharge' (in which people express anger or sadness through listening to music).

Music releases a feel-good neurotransmitter: Salimpoor (2011) found using PET scans that when listening to music, large amounts of dopamine were released, which biologically caused the participants to feel emotions like happiness, excitement, and joy. In 2013, they also found that listening to new music would highly stimulate the nucleus accumbens (the 'reward' circuit of the brain also triggered when eating and having sex) when they enjoyed any of the 60 excerpts of new music.

Music can help people with Alzheimer's disease remember: Some research can be questionable, however if in doubt just watch online. In 2011, the public were introduced to a man in a nursing home, Henry. Initially he showed depressive symptoms before being given an iPod with his favourite music. Immediately he showed a change in character – he was enjoying the music. Afterwards, his clarity in communication and recollection around his youth was very significant. He reacquired his identity for a short time.

Another video, posted by Katie Reed in 2015, shows a segment of an Undergrad capstone by NAU public health students Reed, Adams, Trinidad, and Mcafee. This was a health promotion program that used music therapy with dementia and Alzheimer's patients to increase emotional wellness and memory recall. The difference in wellbeing and lucidity is substantial during and after listening to music.

Short term music training enhances verbal intelligence, memory and problem solving: In 2011, Moreno, Bialystok and Barac found that after only

20 days of training, only children in the music group exhibited enhanced performance on a measure of verbal intelligence, with 90% of the sample showing this improvement. These improvements in verbal intelligence were positively correlated with changes in functional brain plasticity during an executive-function task (memory, problem solving, reasoning, task flexibility). Their findings demonstrated that transfer of a high-level cognitive skill is possible through computerised music training programmes in early childhood.

The Mozart effect is limited: A 1999 study in scientific journal Nature by Chabris, a psychologist, added up the results of 16 studies on the Mozart effect and found only a one-and-a-half-point increase in IQ, and any improvements in spatial ability limited solely to a paper-folding task.

What do these findings mean for schools?

Music clearly has an effect on our mind and also our body. From entering the school, to the time that we leave at the end of the day, pupils are bombarded with different sensory inputs. What these are is up to the school. Take the start of the day, and imagine you are a child who is anxious, depressed or with conduct disorder...

Music in the corridors

Scenario 1: You have a charged state of being, people are all around you in the corridors, and it feels busy, loud and disorganised. People are shouting and jostling. The likelihood is that you would be at risk of not making the correct choices around your behaviour and would be easily agitated.

Scenario 2: Now make the corridors silent. In the background, you hear calming music and the building is carefully lit, tidy and peaceful. Pupils are expected to enter in an orderly manner. The likelihood of you rebounding from any sensory input is diminished, as there is little to rebound from. You are agitated for one reason or another but to greet you is an adult that you know you can trust.

Two very different starts to the day. Music is only one of the sensory inputs within those situations but it can be used to not only play soothing, calm music but to also bring the noise level of others down whilst setting a tone to the day. If you turn around to any headteacher and say install some wireless speakers around our school hotspots and play calming music and the result would be a 30-40% improvement in calmness, you would see a sharp rise in speaker sales for schools. Remember, it worked for tube stations! In turn, you would be more than likely to see improvements in the pupils as they travelled around the school.

Calming music in lessons

As we can see from the study by Chabris, there is very little research proving that the listening of classical music increases IQ. However, classical music during lessons can be calming and soothing to a point. It does depend however on the class you have. Some people like to do things, concentrate or read in silence so be mindful of when to use classical music or another form of background melody. Maths lessons, for example, may increase frustration as they are trying to work out the square root of 324, whereas in an art lesson this may be very beneficial to get the creativity flowing.

Dance

Dance is too underestimated and underexposed within the average school curriculum. Usually covered within the PE curriculum and possibly one, or if you are lucky, two extended school activities, dance is a powerful medium in which children and young people can express themselves and gain confidence.

A recent study (Vordos, Kouidi, Mavrovouniotis *et al*, 2016) found that dancing was a good element of cardiac rehabilitation programme by improving lower limb function. Moreover, and more relevant to our case, the study found that traditional dances contribute to socialisation, reduction of anxiety and mild depression, and improvement of quality of life. In terms of treating psychological and mental health problems, Dance Movement Therapy is quickly becoming a more explored route of supporting people. Throughout all of these, music is used to facilitate and increase the effects along with being a factor in mood enhancement.

There is also the element within many people that they would be too shy to dance in front of others. One of the most primal things that we do can often be a source of anxiety or rejection. Some need copious amounts of alcohol, while some will do it privately. However, Zetner's (2010) findings, based on a study of 120 infants between five months and two years old, suggest that humans may be born with a predisposition to move rhythmically in response to music. They also noted that 'the better the children were able to synchronise their movements with the music, the more they smiled.' So it is a natural, happy thing to do. A school in which children can respectfully dance through the corridors together would be an exceptional place.

Music therapy

During my days in special secondary education we had our own onsite music therapist. She was fully booked throughout the week and was part of a larger therapy unit in which we had three full-time speech therapists via the NHS and an art therapist for one day per week. However, over the years it was the music therapy that made the most difference in the wellbeing and emotions of our non-verbal students. Likewise in the primary setting, music therapy can be very beneficial, usually more than formal counselling for those in early years settings and those with limited speech and communication abilities in later years.

Peripatetic Music lessons and collective experiences

Over the years I have seen a number of children given access to these. Some funded fully by parents, some part-funded by the Pupil Premium fund. One boy when I reflect on this always comes to mind. He was working beneath the expected level and had little in life that made him smile. A part-funded programme of piano lessons was provided and I walked into the hall one day to see how he was doing. I had never seen him so happy – he was beaming like never before, his self-confidence and interest soaring. Such benefits, provided as a standard within many private establishments, should be made further available to those in mainstream schools. In my experience, I have not seen one pupil given the opportunity that did not relish this or feel a sense of achievement when showing others what they had learnt.

The collective experience, being affordable, may have further benefits. Swedish research has suggested that singing within a choir not only increases oxygen levels in the blood but also triggers the release of 'happy' hormones such as oxytocin, which is thought to help lower stress levels and blood pressure. In addition to this, a year-long study on people with mental health problems, carried out by the Sidney De Haan Research Centre for Arts and Health, Canterbury, has also shown that 60% of participants had less mental distress when retested a year after joining, with some people no longer fulfilling diagnostic criteria for clinical depression.

For pupils to embrace music, singing and being part of a bigger thing is something that can only help and develop positive wellbeing. Being part of something even bigger than this as a group – for example, Young Voices at the O2 in London, in which thousands of children come together to sing – has the potential to not only develop wellbeing but also provide memories that define a positive childhood. To positively embrace music in schools has such wellbeing potentials that it should utilised as much as possible. In life it is so deeply embedded within our human nature that is yet to be fully understood. Go on... play the music!

References

Carlson, E, Saarikallio, S, Toiviainen, P, Bogert, B, Kliuchko, M and Brattico, E. (2015): Maladaptive and adaptive emotion regulation through music: a behavioral and neuroimaging study of males and females. *Frontiers Media: Frontiers in Human Neuroscience*. Vol. 9, article no. 466.

Chabris, C. (1999): Prelude or requiem for the 'Mozart effect? Nature Publishing Group: *Nature*. Vol. 400, p. 826-827.

Eerola, P. and Eerola, T. (2013). Extended music education enhances the quality of school life. Sage Publications: *Music Education Research*. Vol. 16, no. 1, p. 88-104.

Harmat, L., Takács, J. and Bódizs, R. (2008). Music improves sleep quality in students. Wiley-Blackwell: *Journal of Advanced Nursing*. Vol. 62, no. 3, p. 327-335.

Moreno, S, Bialystok, E, Barac, R, Schellenberg, G, Cepeda, J, and Chau, T. (2011): Short-term music training enhances verbal intelligence and executive function. *Psychological Science*. Vol. *22*, no. 11, p. 1425-1433.

Music and Memory. (2011): Man in nursing home reacts to music from his era. Available at: musicandmemory.org

Reed, K, Adams, K, Trinidad, A, and Mcafee, K. (2015): The Power of Music in Dementia. Available at: www.youtube.com/watch?v=O5z6pm8M_68

Salimpoor, V, Benovoy, M, Larcher, K, Dagher, A and Zatorre, R. (2011): Anatomically distinct dopamine release during anticipation and experience of peak emotion to music. Nature Publishing Group: *Nature Neuroscience*. Vol. 14, no. 2, p. 257-262.

Salimpoor, V, van den Bosch, I, Kovacevic, N, McIntosh, A, Dagher, A and Zatorre, R. (2013): Interactions Between the Nucleus Accumbens and Auditory Cortices Predict Music Reward Value. American Association for the Advancement of Science: *Science*. Vol. 340, no. 6129, p. 216-219.

Trappe, J. (2009): Music and health-Music and health-What kind of music is helpful for whom? What music not. Deutsche medizinische Wochenschrift. Vol. 134, p. 2601-2606.

Vordos, Z, Kouidi, E, Mavrovouniotis, F, Metaxas, T, Dimitros, E, Kaltsatou, A and Deligiannis, A. (2016): Impact of traditional Greek dancing on jumping ability, muscular strength and lower limb endurance in cardiac rehabilitation programmes. Sage Publications: *European Journal of Cardiovascular Nursing*. Vol. 16, no. 2, p. 150-156.

Zentner, M and Eerola, T. (2010): Rhythmic engagement with music in infancy. National Academy of Sciences: *Proceedings of the National Academy of Sciences*. Vol. 107, no. 13, p. 5768-5773.

'Education breeds confidence. Confidence breeds hope.
Hope breeds peace.' – Confucius (551 BC-479 BC)

CHAPTER 8
Best of British Practice

Jennie Giovanelli, Kingsthorpe College

Context

Kingsthorpe College is larger than the average-sized secondary school, with 1,310 pupils on roll. The proportion of pupils who are from minority ethnic groups is above the national average, as is the proportion of those who speak English as an additional language. The proportion of those pupils who are disadvantaged is average, and the proportion of pupils who have special educational needs and/or disabilities is below the national average. Kingsthorpe College's last full Ofsted inspection was in May 2015 where it was judged as Good in all areas. This was confirmed in a Section 8 inspection in September 2016.

Measure what you value, don't value what you measure

We're all acutely aware of the increasing cuts to school budgets and the diminishing provision for mental health services both nationally and locally. Add to this a context of significant societal change and an ever-moving agenda in the educational landscape, and it's no wonder that schools are experiencing an unprecedented need (and indeed pressure) to support the wellbeing of both their members of staff, and the young people and the communities they serve. However, as a Headteacher of a school whose community faces significant barriers, I feel incredibly privileged to be able to make a difference in spite of all these factors.

For me, this starts with an absolute belief in the power of creating the right culture. A culture that promotes safety and wellbeing at its very heart, sees safeguarding and wellbeing as everyone's business, and values the individual and the transformative power of education and what it should offer to our young people in the very widest sense – beyond just exam results. At Kingsthorpe College, we have a resolute commitment to artistic, athletic and academic excellence, and in order to enable this excellence to flourish, we all have to be passionate and dedicated to developing character. Ensuring this remains important in the College's day-to-day life has to come down to the vision and direction with which I lead the College. It's all too easy to become distracted by the latest initiatives and the lure of undertaking activities that have, at their heart, a motive of ensuring better exam results. However, the reality of doing this is that these activities can often be at the expense of looking after the wider needs of our staff and students.

Of course, culture can be seen as quite nebulous and difficult to pin down, but there are practical strategies that we use at our school to help ensure that an environment is created in which everyone feels valued and able to contribute their feedback.

The KC Playbook

Patrick Lencioni (2012) has written widely on the importance of creating a healthy organisation, and argues that all organisations should be able to articulate answers to six key questions in order to create clarity about what they are trying to achieve:

- Why do we exist?
- How do we behave?
- What do we do?
- How will we succeed?
- What is most important, right now?
- Who must do what?

Each year, we publish our Kingsthorpe College Playbook, which details our answers to Lencioni's six questions:

Kingsthorpe College: Playbook 2017-2018

Why do we exist?
We exist because we believe we are the catalyst in students' artistic, athletic and academic lives.

How do we behave?
We behave with optimism, determination, thoughtfulness and clarity.

What do we do?
We provide character and currency for our students to achieve success.

How will we succeed?
We will differentiate ourselves by creating a healthy organisation that makes student-centric decisions and gives students the opportunities to develop resilience, perseverance and creativity, as well as the ability to be curious, kind and well-rounded individuals.

What is most important, right now?

Thematic goal
Establish a healthy organisation that is whole, consistent and complete where management, operations, strategy and culture fit together and make sense.

Defining objectives:
- Continue to eliminate intradepartmental silos.
- Further improve proactive communication with all stakeholders and recognise that this goes up and down the College.
- Embed and develop work on creating and maintaining highly effective teams.
- Model at Leadership Team level the behaviours and characteristics of a high performing team.
- Insist on visibility and ownership from all leaders at all levels.
- Expect uncompromising aspirations from all those connected with and to the College.

Standard operating objectives:
- Student outcomes.
- Quality of teaching.
- Behaviour and attendance.
- Staff morale and development.

- Student experience.
- Efficiency and effectiveness of support systems.

Start With Why

We also use the principles of Simon Sinek's 2011 book *Start With Why* to represent our priorities and focus for the year. This makes sure that anything we do is streamlined and complements our core purpose. This allows us to filter out 'white noise' and we can make decisions to take actions that are right for our community, our students, and our vision. The visual representation of our school development plan in this way means that we can share and adapt with staff, students, and parents to create a shared vision and understanding. Our commitment to teamwork is paramount and all leaders within the College have their leadership and management performance management target based on building, developing, and sustaining a healthy and high functioning team. This commitment to measuring teamwork is a subtle but important point.

Cascade messages

Lencioni (2012) also highlights the importance of over-communicating and this is something that we have found really helpful in creating a listening culture. A cascade message, sent after every SLT meeting to every member of staff, shares what was discussed in the meeting and any decisions that were made. This contributes to a culture of openness and transparency, and one where there should be no surprises.

Supporting students

At Kingsthorpe College, we subscribe to Sir David Carter's view that sustainable school improvement takes time (2017), and we are lucky to have a Local Governing Board (LGB) who are passionate about providing the very best for our students and local community. The level of critical challenge and support from our LGB means that our long term approach is welcomed and encouraged, but we nevertheless have many practical strategies to support our students that run alongside our commitment to the longer term approach.

Some of the strategies we use include:

- A varied and diverse assembly and PSHE programme that covers all aspects of wellbeing. We have also created a section within our Learning Resource Centre, which mirrors the 'Shelf Help' scheme that has been running in public libraries across the country. Shelf Help is a section in our school library dedicated to books that relate to mental health issues and wellbeing. It provides 13-18-year-olds with a unique catalogue of 35 books recommended by health professionals. In addition, we have found that some of our students engage really well with the 'For me' app launched by the NSPCC as it gives them the opportunity to text rather than talk.

- We have a real focus on e-safety and have been lucky to be able to engage with other local service providers to help offer a range of informative and practical workshops for both students and parents. This included a partnership with our Local Safeguarding Children's Board and the police to screen and share Kayleigh's love story – a short film based on tragic real life events that aims to raise awareness of healthy relationships, safe internet use, grooming and sexual exploitation, as well as where young people can go for help and advice. Following this, school staff and specialist support staff offered a drop in session for our students should they have any concerns following the screening.

- Matching students to tutors and teachers based on connections/appropriate role models – relationships are the cornerstone of our work at the College, and it is important to us that every child feels they have a champion within the school.

- Analysis of patterns of issues presented to see if resources can be targeted and used to support wider community issues – this enables us to creatively use resources given the current economic climate.

- Within our staffing structure, and despite real term cuts in budgets, we prioritise staff equipped to deal with students' wellbeing and provide a school counsellor, family support worker, BEST coordinator (behavioural, emotional and social), and utilise external professionals such as educational psychologists where necessary. We know funding is stretched, but our LGB and senior team are united in the belief that if students aren't emotionally able to engage with their learning because of barriers they face outside of school, we stand no chance of making the difference we know we can when they are in school. This area of staffing need can often be the first thing to go when looking at resources and staffing, but for us this is a short-sighted approach and at odds with our commitment to make sure we leave a legacy of sustainable improvement.

- We also have a good working relationship with our school nurse who runs a weekly drop-in session for all students. From January, she will be delivering a wellbeing programme that will run over five weeks. This programme will cover topics such as relaxation techniques and sleep techniques. This will complement the work that is already being undertaken in our sixth form centre with students on mindfulness, and the importance of both a healthy body and a healthy mind.

- All of our pastoral team are trained in safeguarding at the level of a Designated Safeguarding Lead and whilst again this is at a considerable cost, the first response a student faces when they make a disclosure of any description can be critical. We also offer a range of other provisions relating to aspects of wellbeing such as anger management, self-esteem, and staff who are fully trained in protective behaviour work, and delivering restorative conversations and contracts.

- Transition – we have a first-rate transition programme with a dedicated member of support staff overseeing the entire process, from March of the year that students join us to the end of Year 7. Transition is clearly important in supporting all students but particularly so for the more vulnerable learners who may be joining us. Prior to starting with us, we host a welcome disco for all students, we have opportunities for students to join us on fact-finding sessions after school if they are the only student from their school or feel anxious, we have two transition days for all students with a third for vulnerable students, and a three-day summer school that sees over a hundred of our prospective Year 7s join us. Our Transition Coordinator personally visits every child who is joining us, and spends time talking with them, their school, and parents. As our Transition Coordinator is a support member of staff, she is also able to support our students during the first few weeks both in and out of lessons.

Supporting staff to support students

It can be incredibly hard to empathise and understand the issues related to mental health illnesses if you haven't suffered yourself, and I have a firm belief that we have to equip staff adequately to deal with concerns students might present. Often staff members can think they are being supportive and mean well, but actually –with no deliberate intent – they can say things that trigger a further sense of isolation for young people who are suffering.

Some of the ways in which we try to help our staff to support students are:

- Raising awareness through training, resources, and strategies in our staff bulletin about mental health illness – these are aimed at breaking down stigma and preconceptions. We have a dedicated support member of staff who works with our Designated Safeguarding Lead to implement our wellbeing plan, and she has undertaken the mental health first aid training and will now disseminate this to the wider staff body. In addition, we have already made much use of the Department for Education material published in August 2017.

- We ensure we tailor our training to the roles that staff are carrying out so that everyone is aware of how potential concerns may manifest in each of their particular areas. For example, our canteen staff, reception staff, and Learning Support Assistants are all likely to see different facets of a child's wellbeing, and tailored training enables staff to be better equipped to notice the types of things that may present in their areas. It also helps support the culture that wellbeing is everybody's business.

Supporting staff wellbeing

Over the past couple of years, staff wellbeing has become more and more prominent on social media, amongst Professional Associations, the Department for Education, and most recently we have seen the announcement that a question on staff wellbeing and workload would be added to the Ofsted staff survey. For us at Kingsthorpe College, staff wellbeing goes beyond what can sometimes just be token gestures, and it is part of that listening culture we work hard to maintain and build upon.

Some of the support we offer to staff includes:

- Wellbeing Wednesday: whilst we brand Wednesday as Wellbeing Wednesday and we actively encourage staff to leave on time on this day, it is much more about a commitment to a philosophy and culture amongst the College. This is based on modelling that a work life balance should be promoted and encouraged, and that the College supports a whole variety of ways of working which suit our staff's needs and families. So, for example, some staff choose to leave straight away after school and pick up any work they have to do later in the evening, or staff may choose to stay a bit later and do nothing when they get home. Our email protocol makes very clear that there is no expectation for staff to respond to emails during the evening or at weekends. However, underpinning all of this is the recognition that this aspect is something that is very personal to each and every staff member with some staff, myself included, gaining a tremendous amount of personal enjoyment and challenge from work. What is important to us is that all staff members feel able to have a work/life balance that suits them, and that the College supports this with a commitment to our staff that they can play an active role in their own children's lives by being able to attend special events and so on.

- Supporting staff workload: this goes back to the clarity of communication and the streamlining of priorities and work to ensure that anything we ask of our staff contributes to our core purpose. It is important that my senior team see part of their leadership role as 'thinking' – by this I mean not just accepting whatever happens to be the latest initiative or 'fad' in education, but to filter the huge amount of information out there into what is right for our students and College. The two key questions which always underpin our thinking are 'what will be different?' and 'how will we know?' and we have refined our feedback, homework, data collection, and report systems to make sure that our systems are not disproportionate in terms of workload compared to the impact the work will have on students.

- We provide supervision with an external professional for the members of our pastoral team who deal with safeguarding – this takes place twice a half term to allow them to 'offload' and support their personal wellbeing. We also provide this service to the local primary schools that are in our trust.

- Safeguarding hub – this has been established to facilitate a termly meeting for our Designated Safeguarding Leads of the local schools within our Trust to share common issues and discuss ways in which we can support each other.

- Staff are able to access six free counselling sessions if they require this and time is made for them to attend these. These sessions are paid for from our core budget, but we use Relate to deliver the provision. We have used this to support colleagues who have been diagnosed with depression and anxiety, but we also use it more widely to support members of staff who may be experiencing difficulties such as when returning to a role from maternity leave, or who have suffered the bereavement of a close family member. Provision for talking therapy tends to either be scarce or has a long waiting list yet we know the huge benefits it can bring, and it is therefore important to us that we are able to support our staff in this way.

- A survey (based on the Ofsted staff survey) is undertaken annually to temperature check the culture and climate of the school. All staff are invited to complete this, and it is important to our LGB that this is carried out with transparency and fairness. Our Chair of Governors liaises with a member of the senior team to ensure the process is robust, and results are sent to both him and myself at the same time. As a result of this survey, a 'you said… we did' plan is made.

- A culture of recognition and value is important so for example, using an idea from Chapman and Sisodia (2015), each term my senior team nominate a member of staff who has demonstrated our ways of working (optimism, determination, thoughtfulness, and clarity) and I write to their partners and / or children to let them know why they are such a valuable member of our team.

Ultimately I am clear about my purpose, vision, and what I want for the young people and the community I serve. This means we have to adopt a flexible and needs-driven approach but one that is always underpinned by kindness and decency. Listening to Andy Roe (London Fire Brigade Deputy Assistant Commissioner) at a recent Leading Edge Conference made me reflect on what we mean by resilience. Andy shared that for him resilience was not about stoicism and just getting on with things, it was in fact about openly admitting when we were under pressure and feeling pain.

Surely in recognising our own fragility and encouraging those we work with (students and staff) to do the same, we create a much healthier internal narrative – one where it is all right to admit we are struggling and need help; one where it is acknowledged and modelled to staff and students that we all make mistakes; one where it is acknowledged that in striving for excellence and taking risks, both staff and students will be under pressure and experience failures; and one where people hold themselves and others to account in a caring environment. It is my belief that schools which facilitate the conditions for this are creating truly resilient students and staff.

References

Carter, D. (2017): How do strong schools stay strong?, Talk given at Leading Edge Leadership Conference 9 October 2017.

Chapman, B and Sisodia, R. (2015): *Everybody Matters: The Extraordinary Power of Caring for Your People Like Family.* New York: Penguin.

Department for Education. (2017): Supporting mental health in schools and colleges. Department for Education. Available at: www.education.gov.uk/ (Accessed: 04/09/2017).

Lencioni, P. (2012): *The Advantage: Why Organizational Health Trumps Everything Else In Business.* San Francisco: Jossey-Bass.

Sinek, S. (2011): *Start with Why: How Great Leaders Inspire Everyone To Take Action.* London: Penguin.

'Health is a state of complete physical, mental and social wellbeing and not merely the absence of disease or infirmity.' – World Health Organisation (WHO)

CHAPTER 9
Physical wellbeing

Why is physical wellbeing so important?
Reports by the American College Sports Medicine (Riebe, Thompson and Cotton) have claimed via a range of studies that exercise and regular physical activity at the correct intensity:

- Reduces the risk of heart disease by 40%.
- Lowers the risk of stroke by 27%.
- Reduces the incidence of diabetes by almost 50%.
- Reduces the incidence of high blood pressure, by almost 50%.
- Can reduce mortality and the risk of recurrent breast cancer by almost 50%.
- Can lower the risk of colon cancer by over 60%.
- Can reduce the risk of developing of Alzheimer's disease by a third.
- Can decrease depression as effectively as Prozac or behavioural therapy.

The benefits on long-term health are clear, especially as we get older. A study into causes of death in the United States shows this – I use this only because of the vastness in population, therefore better statistical relevance. Note that obesity was the second highest cause of death, only narrowly topped by smoking. Inactivity and poor diet should arguably, therefore, come with a very large health warning.

You may also wonder, looking below, why the research base is dated back to 2000. The reason for this is to compare to the latest death rates as published by Nicols (2017). There is no significant difference in the causes for the last nearly 20 years – nothing has changed and lessons have not been learnt. In fact, it shows an even poorer picture now than it did 17 years ago. Nearly 75% of all deaths in the US are attributed to just ten causes. The top now, being heart disease (23.4%), then lung cancer (at 160,000) followed by chronic lower respiratory disease (147,000) both linked to smoking. Poor diet and lack of exercise, particularly with heart disease has a large part to play.

As the UK, a smaller statistical base yet similar in lifestyle choices, increasingly moves towards a more sedentary lifestyle and larger portions sizes, the threat of later health problems and poor wellbeing is very real. Coupled with the potential that exercise and good diet has on wellbeing and mental health, schools are in a key position to change viewpoints and later lifestyle choices through purposeful education.

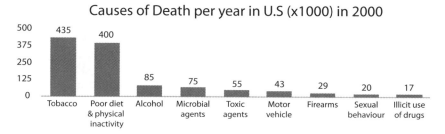

Causes of Death per year in U.S (x1000) in 2000

Source: Mokdad *et al* (2004)

Links to mental health

There is much to be said around developing pupils as healthy learners and improving their mental health and overall wellbeing. The Mental Health Foundation (2017) state that 'a clear distinction is often made between 'mind' and 'body'. But when considering mental health and physical health, the two should not be thought of as separate.' It also outlines how exercise influences the release and uptake of feel-good endorphins in the brain with even a ten-minute brisk walking session increasing 'mental alertness, energy and positive mood'. Diet is also key as 'the food we eat can influence the development, management and prevention of numerous mental health conditions including depression and Alzheimer's.'

Increase of physical activity in schools

Schools over the past decade in particular have been better at providing higher quality physical education with the introduction of the Sports Premium from 2013 and School Games encouraging further competitive sport since 2012. The Olympics, sparking further discussion also helped the nation to embrace sports and athletics in further, more positive ways.

The Children's Health Project – whose work is detailed in Chapter 14 – outline six main learning objectives for healthy eating and movement for schools to aspire to:

- Pupils demonstrate motivation and confidence to engage in daily physical activity
- Pupils are moving for at least one hour a day (moderate to vigorous activity)
- Pupils feel knowledgeable about their body
- Pupils demonstrate an awareness of healthy and less healthy foods
- Pupils make healthy food choices most of the time
- Pupils demonstrate an understanding of how food affects their body, in terms of mood, energy and immunity.

If schools do this, and ensure CYP (Children and Young People) link the benefits with their own mental wellbeing and health, schools would raise cohorts that would potentially embrace healthy lifestyle as a means of self-helping to alleviate depression and improve self-esteem. This can be done in school via a range of channels and methods.

What can schools do?

The Daily Mile or 'Get Up, Get Going': Many schools now take part in The Daily Mile in which pupils run one mile every day over the course of around 15 minutes. One school, Abbotsweld Primary Academy in Essex, have built on this and developed 'Get Up, Get Going (GUGG)' in which pupils are encouraged to get up and moving more throughout the school day to help keep them energised and engaged in their learning. Pupils are rewarded for every ten-minute GUGG period that they complete during the week as well as for a walk to, or from school with recognition for their efforts occurring once they have completed certain milestones.

High quality experiences outside of the normal curriculum: The wider the experiences that can be provided, the better. Schools should aim for every child to be able to name the sport they really like to play and feel happy playing.

The wider curriculum will lead to pupils holding onto the idea that sports and exercise has a huge variety and is enjoyable in different ways. Some will enjoy the feeling of being part of a team, others the personal challenge, another the achievement of hitting that mark. This also includes high quality competitive sports with other schools and challenging pupils to reach higher standards and excellence in specific sports.

Specialist teachers: Primary schools are increasingly looking towards using specialist teachers to enhance provision and provide high quality PPA cover. NET Academies' Harlow Cluster have two highly trained PE teachers delivering PE sessions across their four local schools – as a result, engagement and quality of provision in PE is high. This has led to pupils being more positive around physical exercise and better teaching, learning and training.

Use high quality outside agencies: Sport for Schools is an organisation that helps schools to access inspirational visits from international British athletes from a variety of sporting backgrounds. As part of the half-day visit that each school receives, all pupils get to take part in a fitness circuit and participate in an assembly from the visiting GB athlete.

Another service is Premier Sport that provides taster sessions for a range of sports e.g. archery in which pupils can be given a first experience session. Pupils are taught basic skills of body positioning, how to stand, how to fit an arrow to the bow, aiming and correct releasing technique. As the sessions progress, pupils can also engage in some Level 1 intra-school competition and compete against other members of their class group.

Both of these provide something extra, and different, to inspire even those most hard to reach through high quality coaching experiences.

Boot camps: For those who are less confident and are in need of additional physical sessions, some school provide Boot Camps that provide fun, challenging experiences to motivate and physically challenge. When carefully tracked, pupils can show improvements in fitness and more pride in their physical abilities. This in turn, leads to better engagement and effort in class PE lessons.

Health lifestyle lessons within the primary setting: Lessons allocated specifically to healthy living are beneficial in enhancing understanding around food, exercise and the body. A successful example of this is the Bodycare programme that runs within Essex, providing a health and fitness programme with a range of cross-curricular links, including subjects such as science and mathematics. It is particularly designed for children in Years 4, 5 & 6 to support the curriculum and is delivered by qualified and experienced fitness staff over an eight-week period. Class and specialist teachers can also run these with escalating outcomes over Key Stage 2.

The importance of family involvement

Parents are key determiners in the success of schools developing healthy adults in later life. This ranges from the amount of exercise they take part in, how a family eats and the habits of those around them. Hammons & Fiese (2011) discovered that if a child took part in shared meal times with the family they would be:

- 35% less likely to engage in disordered eating.

- 24% more likely to eat healthier foods.

- 12% less likely to be overweight.

However it is not limited to eating as modelling and guiding children is also imperative. Debbie Mendel (2010) outlined that:

'Children who exercise do better academically and learn how to reduce stress. In essence, adults in the household are showing children a healthy way to relieve stress and improve their thinking while they (the adults) practice what they preach. Children are always observing their parents and picking up on their body language, not just their words.'

Realistically, some families need further support to do this. Below is a practical list of start activities that may help to kick-start families in engaging with healthy lifestyles. This is done best when setting key goals for families and presenting awards/prizes for collective achievements.

1. Parking further away from the school, or even walking the distance – encourage parents to leave the car, walk up the stairs instead of the escalator and carrying light shopping home, rather than taking transport.

2. Burn calories with family dance-offs and competitions to music.

3. Creating a family exercise video – increase fitness when making this then exercise along to the video once made.

4. Set aside 30 minutes per day for exercise – this could be done before dinner, during adverts (collectively), circuits in the living room straight after school, playing football at the local park or going for a walk after dinner.

5. Talk about the benefits of exercise in terms of effects on the body and how you feel mentally afterwards.

6. Create a family Olympics – get inspired by Team GB and join with other friends in the summer to complete your own Olympics. This can even involve the local pool and track.

7. Incorporate home gaming – many gaming systems have a range of games that require movement and competition – from bowling and tennis to snowboarding – have family competitions and consequential exercises for finishing in different places.

8. Plan family picnic days involving outside games such as rounders and cricket.

9. If affordable, buy a family membership at the gym.

10. Gardening can burn 207 calories per hour. Get each family member to plant five plants

11. Washing cars – this could be the neighbours or even the grandparent's.

12. Parkruns – these are local running events in which children and adults run 5k on a Saturday morning. I have seen children as young as eight set a good pace at this distance.

13. If you have a Family Liaison Officer or Support Worker, use some of this time to engage with specific families around their food choices. Those with unhealthy packed lunches or are at risk of obesity in later life are priority.

14. Family challenges to incorporate five fruits and vegetables a day into everyone's diet. Success each week will lead to a treat on a Saturday night.

Throughout all of this, the goal is for exercise and a varied diet being valued as positive, enjoyable aspects to everyday life. When proactively linked to positive mental health by schools, through meaningful and consistent discussion to wellbeing and feeling great, children and young people will have this embedded into their psyche. This way, when it is needed, adults in the next century will hopefully remember these benefits and turn to exercise and diet first to help themselves before it potentially escalates to depression or worse.

References

Hammons, J and Fiese, B. (2011): Is Frequency of Shared Family Meals Related to the Nutritional Health of Children and Adolescents? in *Pediatrics*. Illinois: The American Academy of Pediatrics. Vol. 127, no. 6.

Mendel, D. (2010): *Addicted to Stress: A Woman's 7 Step Program to Reclaim Joy and Spontaneity in Life*. New Jersey: Jossey-Bass.

MHO. (2017): Physical health and mental health. Available at: www.mentalhealth. org.uk/a-to-z/p/physical-health-and-mental-health

Mokdad, A et al (2004) 'Actual Causes of Death in the United States, 2000' - *JAMA (Journal of American Medical Association),* March 10, 2004 – Vol 291, No. 10, p.1239

Nichols, H. (2017): The top 10 leading causes of death in the United States. *Medical News Today.* Available at www.medicalnewstoday.com/articles/282929. php

Riebe, D, Thompson, P and Cotton, R. (2014): ACSM Exercise is Medicine – Factsheet. Available at: exerciseismedicine.org/assets/page_documents/EIM%20 Fact%20Sheet%202014.pdf

'It's absolutely crucial to confront problems as early as possible to prevent them from escalating into even greater issues in later life.' – Duchess of Cambridge, 2016 Place2Be Wellbeing in Schools Awards

CHAPTER 10
Best of British Practice

Gillian Kierans, Headteacher, Aultmore Park Primary and LCR

Aultmore Park Primary and LCR was formed eight years ago in the Easterhouse area of Glasgow. It is the sixth most deprived school in Glasgow and is situated within the tenth most deprived area in Scotland. It is estimated that 98% of the pupils live in poverty in the area.

When we amalgamated, behaviour was extremely challenging and we experienced very high levels of violence and aggression between and from pupils. Over the first full school year, we had the highest exclusion rate within the city and learning and teaching suffered as a result.

I sought out the support of Place2Be during that first year as it was clear that we were unable to provide the emotional support required by the children. Issues they were sharing with us included domestic violence, neglect, physical abuse, parental drug and alcohol misuse and bereavement as well as friendships and peer relationships.

As Place2Be became embedded within the school, we embarked on an ongoing programme of professional development with all staff in the school; teachers, Support for Learning workers (SfLW), clerical, catering and janitorial, to ensure all staff were responding to the pupils in a way which supported their emotional development.

Staff development was key in the transformation that took place over the next few years. We worked on developing The Six Principles of Nurture with a particular focus on developmental learning and all language being seen as communication. Too often, we were reacting to the behaviour, rather than trying to understand what lay behind the behaviour and what the child was trying to tell us. Place2Be provided training for staff throughout the school year. The School Project Manager provided additional support to the Senior Management Team, helping them to work through issues being experienced by both pupils and staff.

What are the six principles of nurture?

- Children's learning is understood developmentally.

- The classroom offers a safe base.

- Nurture is important for the development of self-esteem.

- Language is understood as a vital means of communication.

- All behaviour is communication.

- Transitions are significant in the lives of children.

We established an ongoing programme specifically targeted at our Support for Learning Workers. Their job is to support the most challenging of pupils throughout the school day, working with them in class and on a one-on-one basis, providing support for learning as well as emotional and behavioural support. We also recognised that they required additional training as they support the children in the playground, and in some respects, this is where the children display the most challenging behaviours. They are in an unstructured environment and are responsible for regulating their own behaviour, as well as managing peer relationships. In a playground of 300 pupils, this can prove to be very difficult for many pupils. Senior managers were dealing with numerous incidents at every break that took up most of their day-to-day working. There was signification disruption to learning and teaching and staff morale was low.

Place2Be worked with our SfLW on a variety of topics – Supporting Children in the Playground, Attachment Theory, Behaviour as Communication, Child Development and Play Therapy to name a few. Staff reported that their understanding of children's development increased, both physically and emotionally. They learned new strategies and ways to respond to the behaviours presented by the pupils. Children began to be understood developmentally and their emotional wellbeing was now at the front of interactions. We invited other SfLWs to some of our trainings and our staff were able to share their successes with their colleagues.

Place2Be continue to provide training for teachers and SfLW throughout the school year. Staff understanding and knowledge of emotional wellbeing and mental health has increased. Staff regularly refer pupils to Place2Talk for the valuable solution focussed support provided by our School Project Manager. All staff are asked for their thoughts and recommendations for pupils who would benefit from their 1-1 service, which can provide up to a year's therapeutic support. Our relationships with partner agencies such as CAMHS have developed and all of our referrals to this service are accepted as our understanding of their criteria for mental health interventions has improved and they know the level of support and interventions provided for the pupil is of a very high standard.

'Children who are distracted and unable to deal with their worries will not be able to engage with their learning and reach their full potential. We all need good mental health to engage positively with our lives, have a sense of hope and optimism and develop the resilience we need to cope with life's problems.' – Dame Benny Refson, President, Place2Be.

Our school is a very different place now than it was eight years ago. Our exclusion rates have reduced year on year and our attainment has continued to increase. All pupils make progress every year. Visitors comment upon the excellent manners and behaviour of our pupils. Staff morale has increased and our school has been nominated for and won numerous awards. Staff are responsive to the emotional wellbeing of pupils and this is at the forefront of our practice. With the support of Place2Be, we are more able to look after the mental health and wellbeing of our pupils and give them support when they need it, in a safe environment that allows them to progress and flourish and achieve their potential.

References
Refson, B. (2016): Why Support Children's Mental Health In Schools? New York: *Huffington Post*. Available at: www.huffingtonpost.co.uk/dame-benny-refson/place2be-wellbeing-in-school-awards_b_13124886.html

'Social Media has become a space in which we form and build relationships, shape self-identity, express ourselves, and learn about the world around us; it is intrinsically linked to mental health.' –Shirley Cramer CBE, Royal Society for Public Health (RSPH)

CHAPTER 11
E-safety and social media

The dangers and effects of the Internet, and our lives increasingly being on digital platforms, has had significant effects on both adults' and children's wellbeing over the last ten years. It is not likely to go away and will become even more prevalent in the next ten years. Out of the total 7.2 billion people on this planet, three billion use the internet with 1.7 billion of these having social networking accounts.

There are stark negatives to technology. For example, Sean Parker, former president of Facebook who joined Mark Zuckerberg in its first few months, recently attacked Facebook for 'exploiting a vulnerability in human psychology'. He stated that 'it probably interferes with productivity in weird ways. God only knows what it's doing to our children's brains'. There are also the risks of online bullying, sharing too much information, exposure to inappropriate content and vulnerability to predatory adults.

However, there are also great positives: social groups for new mums, WhatsApp groups for parents, the new #joinin Twitter campaign for people that are alone finding company. Much of this comes down to using social media positively and approaching it with a healthy and safe mindset. Social media also helps people to stay connected with one another e.g. children who do not live with both parents or have loved ones abroad, developing new contacts with peers who have similar interests and using platforms to express interests and developing their identities.

In the midst of all this is the case around wellbeing and mental health of CYP and what schools should do.

Some statistics...
YoungMinds (2017) state that:

- Children and young people spend an average of 12 hours a week online.
- One in three 11-16-year-olds have been targeted, threatened or humiliated online.
- Not all young people who are vulnerable online appear so in other aspects of their lives, suggesting that online risks can show up in unexpected ways.
- A quarter of UK children in a 2014 survey reported skipping meals or sleep because of the internet.

The statistics are likely to be more realistic and less controversial than some found in the media, however if you searched you would find many shocking claims. From the above we can see that CYP are online for a few hours per day and a significant proportion have either been bullied online or are not managing their sleep appropriately due to Internet usage. This is a fair assumption to make, however there are further realistic risks that we as schools must consider.

What risks do children and young people face when using the internet and how does it affect wellbeing?
From the age of around 11-12 young people in general are at a greater risk. They move to secondary school, open to new social groups and before they know it have a new found freedom and social life. Today's technology more than often facilitates these social circles, and the threat of FOMO (Fear Of Missing Out) will undoubtedly be a key reason as to why CYP want certain applications. This in itself is not too dissimilar to 25 years ago in which you would use the only phone in your house, much to your parent's frustration, and talk for hours to your friends, boyfriends, girlfriends etc. There was no trail for parents to see. There were no message threads or logs. So what has changed?

For schools, there is the added dimension of 'open use' that is more of the issue. No longer are the conversations directly between two people or people that are well known to that person. This has created a range of scenarios and opportunities that can affect wellbeing and mental health:

- Group chats leading to deformation of character and/or cyber bullying.
- Image-based abuse in which intimate or sexual photos are shared online without consent, usually to humiliate someone or for entertainment of others.
- Social media pick me ups – seeking external validation through photos, blogs and videos. This can develop negative self-image when not liked enough or negative comments made.
- Easy access to illegal content via gaming, internet searches, use of inappropriate apps and programmes.
- Sexting.

With technology at their fingertips, CYP are more likely to place themselves at risk from one of the above without ongoing education in schools.

Children as young as ten are now immersing themselves in an open online lifestyle, for example, using Instagram to gain followers, attempting to get more than 1000 likes in Musical.ly. The open use in which CYP are openly sharing themselves with unknown people places them at greater risk for a range of reasons:

1. It places them in direct contact with unknown people, including a real risk of adults for sinister purposes. This may include the sending of inappropriate messages and images.

2. Peers may potentially make unkind comments online – privately or publicly – that will affect self-esteem and image.

3. Scenarios around the need of a specific number of likes increases addiction to apps and can potentially lead to further open use and risky behaviours to increase likes and attention for self-validation. This is alike to some adults when blogging i.e. why did I only get 88 likes for this piece, the last got 420 – why did they not like it? What did I do wrong? Cases in which CYP place riskier photos and videos can lead to further attention from paedophiles and unwanted feedback from peers.

4. Many apps are not easy to navigate for adults who are fresh to the app. For example, if a child messaging privately an unknown adult on

Instagram with the messaging function unknown to parents. These scenarios are commonly later shared by peers who decide a teacher should know when the situation gets too serious.

5.   Staying online till late at night on phones or tablets whilst chatting online. The lack of sleep will affect concentration and over time mood, concentration and resilience. This can lead to insomnia if pupils are becoming addicted to app use and late night notifications.

6.   An increase in secrecy and a further closure of face-to-face socialising out of school. When developing into compulsive use, CYP may develop depression or loneliness.

7.   Lack of physical activity. With increasing convenience in communication and sharing apps, CYP can talk to people without getting out of bed or meeting friends in person. The lack of physical movement can lower metabolism and feel good chemicals within the body. This can get worse in CYP become compulsive regarding their online world.

8.   Lack of family time through replacing with an online 'family'. In the most extreme cases, CYP are open to grooming and extremism via forums and meeting strangers across a number of apps. Again, secrecy revolving around these can be well hidden and difficult to detect by parents and teachers.

9.   Sharing of private information – particularly in recent years for app gifts. Parents must be aware that online gaming – even those not deemed a social threat such as FIFA 18 – has the option of gifting players and certain game elements to other users. During matches CYP can talk via headset or direct messaging on e.g. Xbox One. Strangers can therefore start potential 'online friendships' and then invite them to use other online platforms for more access, including role-play.

Why should we embrace technology and not limit it?

1.   The use of apps and online programmes

Technology is still very new to our society and is growing quicker than society can manage – adults are not keeping up with the pace of social media platforms and the individual dangers within these. Children on the other hand are very nimble and adept at mastering the devices and uses of apps as they have grown using these from earlier ages.

Last year we brought in the 'Two Johns' (EST Training) to work with all pupils from ages 5-11. They showed an image on the screen of characters from Roblox, an online gaming programme in which people can talk freely to strangers. Over 50% of pupils knew the characters and what the programme was... this was in Year 1! The startling thing was that none of our parents, when shown the same picture knew these and many did not know their children were using it.

Naturally, the knee-jerk reaction by some is to close off media apps and to restrict this. The advice was, if you can make it safe then do so. If not, then an informed stopping of the app would be best – by that, children talk to an adult about the dangers of the app, the adult discusses the pros and then dangers of this. The CYP then makes an informed choice as to whether they really should use this – praise is given for when they make the right decision to stop the dangerous app. The method around this is that a direct adult-led ban is likely to move children into more secretive actions and measures to continue. Talking through scenarios is also best.

2.   Online counselling and support

The use of technology can enhance wellbeing – services such as Samaritans (since 1953) and Childline (since 1986) have provided distance services for a number of years, and have done this well. As a nation however we have not entirely used technology to its full potential for positive wellbeing gains. Many services within healthcare settings are limited in time and capacity. Technology can be used to enhance these services and there is a need to further signpost support for those that can use it.

Recently, on the London Underground I saw a poster on the signposting people to use an app to speak to a qualified doctor. I gave this a go and saw a doctor online within ten minutes at the cost of £20 – it even allowed me the option of signing in using Facebook. The University of Sheffield have recently opened CATCH (Centre for Assistive Technology and Connected Healthcare) that are researching, evaluating and implementing 'new technologies to enable people to live well and age well'. This ranges from dementia to sight loss – the fact is that technology services is rapidly growing. Many of our CYP need to maintain and enhance their multi-media use in order to later reach and make best use of services on a range of platforms – this will include wellbeing and mental health services to provide rapid care and support.

3.   The Kooth Model

The recent report by the Education Policy Institute 'Online Mental Health Support for Young People' focused on the Kooth Model – an online counselling and emotional wellbeing platform for children and young people. One of the most prominent findings from the report were the age range of those using the service as:

> 'The median age of a Kooth service user is 15, which reflects the pattern of emergence of mental health problems in young people aged between 14 and 17. Nearly one in five (18%) of the new registrations in 2016-17 were for those aged between 10 and 12, showing that online provision of mental health support is popular with pre-teenage children as well as teenagers.'

This raises the question for not only secondary schools but also that of primary as to how these services are signposted and accessed for those who need it. Additionally, it was found that girls were more likely to use the online service (71% being girls or young women), whereas boys preferred face-to-face counselling. It also found that boys are likely to use the service at a younger age and may indicate that older teenage boys are less likely to engage with mental health support or to engage with such support online.

There is also the additional factor of the type of service accessed (the most common reason for accessing being stress and anxiety, along with bullying, relationships, self-harm and lack of self-worth):

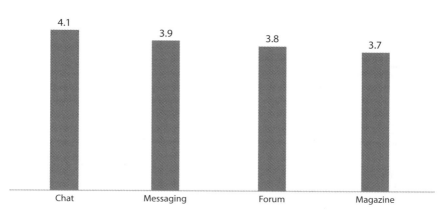

Client appreciation of elements of Kooth Model
(Score out of five)

The types of services that should be signposted in secondary schools and colleges, due to the clear split between preferences, is also to be very well thought out by institutions. In addition, and of interest, is the 'goal achievement by category' and the success in obtaining the goal. EPI (2017) noted that:

'goals in relation to learning difficulties saw the most progress whereas 'fitting in' saw the least. A high level of progress was seen in goals based on suicidal thoughts. Goals focused on specific behaviours such as smoking, anger management or self-harm saw less progress overall.'

This places into question the effectiveness of different online methods and the range of mental health needs it can cater for. It also on the other hand raises the importance of embracing technology and how this can proactively support the most vulnerable who may not access help or be given quick enough provision.

Recording of e-safety concerns at school

The recording of e-safety concerns is also essential for schools to track and monitor concerns. If you do not already do so via an online recording system, log and detail e-safety concerns separately to track individuals or trends. A form such as the one below will help you do this:

Date of Incident/Concern	Child/Children	Year Group	
What has happened? What was disclosed?			
What is the nature of the concern? Please tick below.			
Cyber Bullying (Use of technology to bully a person or group with the intent to hurt them socially, psychologically or even physically).			
Image-based abuse (When intimate or sexual photos or videos are shared online without consent, either to humiliate or shame someone, or for the 'entertainment' of others).			
Access to offensive or illegal content – this includes access to games that are not appropriate for the age of the child.			
Sexting (The sending of provocative or sexual photos, messages or videos. They are generally sent using a mobile phone but can also include posting this type of material online).			
Social Networking – including the negative use of social media and access to apps that are inappropriate			

Trolling/Damage to digital reputation (Trolling is when a user anonymously abuses or intimidates others online for fun. They purposely post inflammatory statements, not as a way to bully or harass other people, but to watch the reactions. Damage to digital reputation can also occur by people that are known to the child).
Unwanted contact (Any type of online communication that they find unpleasant or confronting. This also includes contact with strangers online).
Other (please state):

What is the outcome? What decisions and actions have been made?
Have parents been informed?   **Has the class teacher been informed?**
What was the outcome of the conversation with parents?
Name of person completing initial record: _____ **Date:** _____
Handed to and completed by (SLT member): _____ **Date:** _____

It is important to note that when disclosures are made, the guidelines are the same for other safeguarding scenarios. However there is the added complexity in enabling children and families to be further supported. A proactive way of doing this is through opening online surgeries.

Online surgeries

Schools are often faced with difficult scenarios that have developed outside of the school setting, yet include those from the school e.g. online bullying via Instagram or image-based abuse via Snapchat. Sarah Brennan, Chief Executive of YoungMinds, states that:

'Our research shows that children and young people understand the online world a lot better than most adults, they are active creators of content, and are discerning when it comes to navigating social media. They're more likely to listen to other young people, including older siblings, than adults warning them about the dangers of the online world.'

We need to keep this in the forefront of our minds. CYP are not freely going to their parents or coming forward as much as we would like when they need help.

One positive way to tackle this is through online surgeries. Pupils can openly come to a room at lunchtime to talk to older peers and/or trusted adults about online problems and to discuss their app settings. This is in a non-judgemental environment in which pupils can be advised how best to keep themselves safe. Through correct marketing to the school community, pupils can feel that it is grown up and responsible to actively talk about it. Where parents need to be informed, an agreement that open discussion and praise for asking for help is to be encouraged. This way, pupils will develop assurance that open discussion is positively acknowledged rather than pushing the subject under the radar of adults.

How can schools support parents and CYP?

Schools can further support pupils and parents to work towards better wellbeing and safety by:

- Open discussions around certain apps and online programmes. Discuss and help CYP to either change the app settings or make an informed decision to delete an app that cannot be adapted for their own safety. Not all CYP will immediately delete the app, however the positive reinforcement of those that initially do will encourage more to do the right thing.

- Focus on apps that have most potential for pupils to be contacted by strangers i.e. Musical.ly, Live.ly, Roblox, StackPlant, Minecraft, Snapchat, Instagram.

- Educate parents to help keep children safe online – buy in external providers to give after school talks – market this extensively using statistics and key questions around popular apps to get the parents talking.

- Introduce parents/carers to ideas such as 'Electronic Free Sundays' for families – starting at an early age bring back core family time, not only for children to play in other ways but to stop parents from looking at their phones and to spend quality time with their children.

- A mindset of 'protect', rather than 'control' is key in tackling the use of online communication. Instil good practices early on – setting key messages to children from a young age regarding responsibility and keeping safe.

- Look out for compulsive behaviour. Questionnaires for CYP and parents can develop a picture regarding online use, the time they spend and apps used.

- Remember that intensive parenting and parental surveillance of online use is effective only up to a point. CYP are far more adept at using digital materials.

- Work with teenagers about 'owning the apps, rather than them owning you'. Openly teach changing app settings so that they are healthy in lifestyles e.g. not living on notifications – the push of social validation by the app continuously beholds the user to the app. When not getting these can feed negatively as they are not getting feedback. This also interrupts normal everyday actions.

- Remember that this is also essential for all staff to know – staff training can make a large difference to creating open discussions.

References

Field, M. (2017): Former Facebook president Sean Parker: 'God only knows what it's doing to our children's brains'. Available at: www.telegraph.co.uk/technology/2017/11/10/ex-facebook-president-sean-parker-god-knows-childrens-brains

YoungMinds (2017): Life on the Web. Available at: youngminds.org.uk/get-involved/campaign-with-us/life-on-the-web

Frith, E. (2017): Online Mental Health Support for Young People. Education Policy Institute. Available at epi.org.uk/report/online-mental-health-support

'The children now love luxury. They have bad manners, contempt for authority; they show disrespect for elders and love chatter in place of exercise.' – Socrates (470 BC-399 BC)

CHAPTER 12
Staff Wellbeing – Dear Leadership Team...

If you are a school leader... read this. If you are not – photocopy the chapter and leave it on the desk of your most active senior leader. Reckon they will start the ball rolling on at least two of these within a week!

Dear Leadership Team,

Please read the below – it has some interesting ideas...

The importance of staff wellbeing cannot be underestimated. The National Audit Office (NAO) in 2016 reported that teachers leaving the profession between 2011 and 2014 had increased 11% over three years. Those leaving ahead of retirement increased from 64% to 75%. In addition, it suggested that schools in poorer areas found attracting and keeping good teachers more difficult (54% in comparison to 33% in less disadvantaged schools). 40% of teachers leave the profession within the first five years of starting.

The typical experience of a school leader when recruiting has vastly changed in the last five years from having nearly 20 good applicants per position to none – having to actively seek or 'grow their own', by recruiting graduates and starting from scratch with Schools Direct placements. Retention of staff is therefore vital for schools and ensuring teaching remains at a sustained good or better. Any headteacher may tell you that the following equation applies. Happy staff = retention = better, more consistent learning for pupils. So how do you retain staff and achieve the best out of your team?

One thing needs to be made clear...
The ideas set out are no replacement for the importance of ethos and culture in the school. The behaviour of leaders ensures the formation of positive, meaningful bonds across the school. This is imperative to having a successful thriving school in every sense of the word. The buy-in to the school, its goals and way of being cannot be replaced by initiatives. However, there are things that do go down well and aid in having a great wellbeing package.

Acknowledgement and respect for all
The headteacher and senior leaders acknowledging the efforts of all of those in the team is by far the most effective way of raising staff wellbeing. Communication with all staff and recognition of their achievements is key.

Be smart about workload and expectations (also see 'lower the burden of marking and planning')
As a school define what is most important and what teachers expect. So many new teachers ask me during their interview or shortly afterwards what it is that I am looking for or expect from them – keep it simple and clear. For example, we ask teachers to only concentrate on our 5 Bs:

- Books
- Behaviour
- Base (classroom)
- Bonds (positive relationships with staff and pupils)
- Best practice

High quality training
Not directly relating to 'wellbeing' but teachers and support staff do enjoy, and respect, high quality INSET days and weekly training, In addition, the best schools map out a development package to provide to all staff across all levels. From opportunities to courses to qualifications, if staff are aware that they have a development pathway, they are more likely to feel better about their careers and will want to stay for the next step.

Never mention the 'O' word

For the majority of schools, Ofsted are in a school setting for 1 in every 1000 days and should be treated as such. Nothing should be done because of them or for them. In recent years – since the 2015 overhaul and particularly through the positive voice of Sean Harford – Ofsted regularly stated schools should not do anything outside of their common practice for inspections and this includes marking, planning and practice. As such school leaders should not deem a visit as a problem for any staff – it is for leaders to deal with, not teachers or support staff to worry about.

Star days

If your staff have 99-100% attendance (the equivalence of two days illness) in a year, have shown great impact over the year and have worked well, then a day off to see their little one performing in a play or to have an extended break over the weekend is a great way of acknowledging their efforts and commitment. Some schools do this formally as a scheme, others less so with the assurance that if you meet set criteria this is open for the day or two of your choice.

Health insurance and wellbeing packages

If you are part of an MAT (Multi-Academy Trust), it is certainly easier to get great deals. Our current insurance provider also gives the staff a 'Wellbeing Package' that includes up to £300 physio, free pair of glasses every two years, stress counselling and even a wellbeing app. Schools can also buy into health insurance for staff as part of employment and retention packages.

Lunches together

'First Friday Fest' we call it, as it happens on the first Friday of each month. Call it what you will, but there is certainly a good vibe when everyone pitches in and brings something to a table to be together. Some make great homemade items such as sausage rolls or banoffee pie that staff eagerly scramble around until next month – others buy something tasty from the local shop. Again, it is something to look forward to as a collective.

Look at your timetable

Academies have the ability to change the times and days in which pupils attend school. However, by the end of 2014, 'just 19% of academies have changed, or were intending to change the length of the school day, while only 6% have altered their term times.'

Some schools (academies) now decide that a longer school day is more beneficial for an improved timetable and learning opportunities. By extending the school day by 30 minutes, the number of weeks at school drops from 39 to 36. The educational advantages for children are an enhanced timetable and opportunities, along with a standardisation of term lengths – say goodbye to the long summer term! The advantages for teachers are an additional three weeks of rest and reflection.

Flexibility

We all have lives outside of school – our children's school performances, a wedding of a close friend, time to grieve over the anniversary of losing a loved one, that concert that only comes up once every eight years, a few hours to get off early to see your eldest fly off to Australia for a year. There are so many reasons our mind may go to something other than school. Be flexible and allow for staff to have time where it is possible.

Dress down Fridays

On the last Friday of half term – the children and staff hold a non-uniform day, raising money for different charities – this not only keeps the children excited and attendance high but also enables staff to wear more comfortable clothing. We finish the Friday at 5pm with a curry at our local. The finish at 5pm is a genuine finish. Marking is done, classrooms are prepped and everyone leaves knowing that they have a great half term without any work. We all agree that the curry tastes far better with the knowledge that we have a genuine week or two off.

International programme

Over the past few years I have seen colleagues sent abroad to study and discover best practice across the globe. Some of the greatest were Hong Kong to look at reading, Finland to study effective Early Years provision, mathematics in Switzerland and computing in the Netherlands. A trip to the U.S to visit Google's offices and get new ideas for educational and thinking environments would be a high one on the list. These trips can be funded outside of the school's budget, though outreach work for other schools and organisations. The payback... something most schools do not offer – to see the best in the world and to bring it back to yours. It creates a great vibe with staff and those who go never forget who sent them.

Open door policy

Do not do this! Confused? Don't be! As a head if you have an open door policy you will never get anything done – there are times when you need to get things done, like anyone else in the school. However, make sure you are available at key times when people may need you. Make sure you are clear about when you are free e.g. having the door open, when it is okay to talk and give 100% attention.

Gym package or classes for teachers

Teaching is, and can be, very stressful. I was lying down and looking at the roof of the swimming pool in my local gym thinking how lucky I was to have access to such amenities. Imagine the teaching staff's reaction to having a gym membership courtesy of the school. I know what you are thinking... how do you suggest we do this with the current austerity? This depends on your locality. There are no-frills gyms that cost around £25 per month, all the way to more luxury ones costing £100. If you can find a mid-priced gym at around £50 per month this will cost you £600 per person – less than one pay increment.

The point is this that not all teachers will take you up on the offer, but those that do will relate feeling good, losing weight and better wellbeing with the school directly as a result. It is hard to leave a school, but even harder to leave a gym that is free! In short – happier staff leads to better retention. You will save money on less job advertising.

If this is not a viable option then look at those around you. Is there a trained instructor in the midst? I taught weekly legs, bums and tums classes and a weight-based workout – this added depth to the school's extra-curricular programme and was open to all staff for just £2 per week to cover insurance and equipment cost. Alternatively, you can all chip in and get a Zumba coach! The collective feel is something that cannot be replicated.

Nights out and events
Get someone on the staff to be the events coordinator. Whether it is a Tough Mudder obstacle course, a drink after work, Turkish meal, night out at a 70s Soul Bar or a West End show with cocktails – make sure that the events cater for all tastes over time and for all budgets. The consistent programme of events generates discussion and unknown friendships that span across status. Some schools have an event at their local establishment every Friday, others once a half term – keep it updated, consistent and well promoted.

Refreshment facilities
Tea and coffee, and the odd biscuit, is basic essentials in a staffroom.

Cold water
It sounds like an obvious thing – however it was the number one request from my staff last year! Plumbed in water coolers can cost as little as £20 per month.

Never grade lessons
Those lessons that are amazing and provide pupils with such memorable experiences, yet they do not tick a certain box or are only deemed as making 'good' progress... Don't do that. Simply contextualise what benefitted learning and what would have helped it further. Grading lessons affects staff wellbeing and morale. It is also not conducive to a positive staff mentality around development.

Therapeutic buy-ins

Give staff the opportunity to access therapeutic amenities and relate wellbeing directly with 'work'. Some recent ideas were 'Fingertip Fridays' in which a nail technician visits once a month and all staff can access this during staggered breaks and lunch, leaving the school with a new set of acrylics or shellacs. Another example is having a massage company deliver office chair, desk or Indian head massages – these need no oil and can be delivered in ten minutes. Walk away after a week at work with new gels and a head massage... more than likely to put a smile on people's faces and raise happiness and retention. It costs the school nothing but, by organising, it lets everyone know you care.

The staffroom

We are in the midst of revamping the staffroom – it is agonising! We have gone through everything from a café style bistro to a lounge chair enclosure. Reduce the possibility of cliques by thinking carefully about layout and make this a place where all staff will want to go and need to get to, rather than diving out the gates to get away or eating in their cars.

Lower the burden of marking and planning – introduce conferencing

Ensure the marking policy is clear but not demanding. In 2016, the Education Endowment Foundation (EEF) reported that there was markedly little evidence or relevant research to suggest that detailed or extensive marking has any significant impact on pupils' learning. Leaders only need to ensure that everyone is following the assessment/marking policy – as such make the policy simple and marking less. Cut down arduous marking and bring in conferencing (one-on-one and small group discussions to provide next steps). This is more effective in moving learning forward and reduces the burden on teachers.

Some schools have set their policy as doing just conferencing – if this aids learning and everyone can do this effectively then why not? Spending time with pupils discussing their learning also helps to enhance communication between teacher and pupil, thus building further positive relationships and wellbeing.

Coaching

Training key people to be coaches for teams of teachers may seem a bit odd. However, the benefits can be huge for both the school and staff. In providing teaching staff with a series of confidential one on one sessions with a staff member who is not a line manager to reflect on practice, their position and the school can considerably help with reflection and perspective in their role and next steps.

An alternative approach would be to buy-in a professional coach, starting with the leadership members, for group and individual sessions. This enables the team and individuals to effect on current issues, communication and how they fit into the whole picture. This develops a sense of self and can transform the way in which leaders approach wider school aspects and have a positive effect to all.

Team building INSETs

These are a great way to start the academic year – you will have new staff joining and wondering what you are all about. You can hold a relatively cost-free day by doing activities such as:

- Paper fashion show: groups must create an outfit out of paper and tape for one member of the team – finishing with a catwalk style show.
- Create the highest tower: again only tape and newspapers are needed OR marshmallows and spaghetti.
- Desert Island survivors: teams find five objects within the school they would like to use in order to survive. The activity leader then decides, based on their choices, who would survive the longest.
- Obstacle course: this does not have to be physically demanding – a simple course with activities that can be accessed by all but needs teamwork would suffice.
- Egg drop: provide the staff with two sheets of paper, six straws and some tissue. Find out who can drop the protected egg from a high place (first storey window) without it smashing.

It is important when doing these activities that groups are carefully selected – a range of roles, social circles and personalities can really make a difference. Each of these activities can take around 30 minutes – if introduced with a range of good speakers, bringing your core values to the forefront, staff will finish the day feeling energised and ready for the term.

TeachMeets

TeachMeets are a fantastic way of raising the excitement levels of being in the profession and developing all staff. The short presentations – usually two to seven minutes – allow for space in between to really get the staff enthused and feel valued. Contact a range of local organisations, such as supply agencies, local businesses, even the local supermarkets. Ask them to donate what they can – electronic devices, vouchers, books, gadgets. You can even throw in an afternoon at home – these are all things that can be handed out whilst in between speakers to create a real sense of enjoyment and togetherness. Your staff will remember it and feel valued with great ideas and prizes. Get involved.

Cannot wait to see what is in store for us!

Best wishes,

Your Hard-Working Staff

'Maybe you have to know the darkness before you can appreciate the light.' – Madeline L'Engle

CHAPTER 13
Chalkface Survivors: Leadership with PTSD

A Deputy Headteacher in London

I consider myself a normal person.

I consider myself to have had a loving childhood.

I consider myself to be a conscientious teacher and an even better deputy headteacher.

I consider myself also to be very lucky in comparison to millions in this world.

So why, at the age of 29, was I hanging with a rope around my neck?

The answer to that was not as simple as I thought.

The knot at the top of the bannister came apart and I hit the floor with an almighty crash. I mean, I wanted to die, but I didn't plan on hurting myself – you see there's a difference.

Before climbing over and lowering down the stairwell I didn't write a letter as I had lost contact with my family about two years before this. There were occasional discussions and the odd visit for birthdays, but to me they were too far away for me – mentally and emotionally – to reach out to. My then husband was not at home and after years of being controlled and emotionally and physically abused; I had nothing left to say to him. It is the strangest feeling to be at peace with your own mortality and truly not care about your existence. You can no longer be hurt and nothing around you matters. It was, for me, the act of having control over something – my choice about me.

I climbed the stairs again, cursing my lack of ability for knot tying. I tried again. This time it was the spindle that broke. Again, there was more swearing and, once the pain had subsided, laughter. At that point, the situation was so bad that it was comical.

When teaching, nothing else in the world mattered. I was considered as one of the best teachers in a very large school and, as head of my department, was well respected. Although inside I felt depressed, I somehow still functioned at school – it gave me a sense of being myself but as soon as I got home I was isolated and alone. I was not allowed to go out or make new friends but it was something that I was used to. I wasn't even aware that it was wrong or that I was missing so many things in life.

I was a non-practising Christian – I don't know whether that is a good or bad thing. I did wonder whether things happen for a reason but lost much faith over the years. After the suicide attempt, I didn't know what to do next and it took me a couple of months to figure out that I really did have to leave the relationship. The break-up took its toll on me over the initial months – my headteacher was very understanding and supportive and he helped me stay on track and keep to deadlines. Inside, it took me the next ten years to rebuild myself, my family and friendships and a sense of wellbeing in myself to get back to the real 'me' from long ago. And I thought, at that point, I was okay.

It was only after another seven years, and a bereavement of a loved one, that I started to shut down at work and home. My friend was the one in the end to break the ice and tell me I needed help, as I seemed depressed. It was hard for me to hear and took me a long while to rationalise a polite response but I figured it was probably hard for her to say it too!

Over the course of months, I saw more of a light. I gained a better understanding of why I was like I was – stemming back, would you believe, from childhood and relationships. For years I had suffered from depression, I was scared to admit it and feared that any medication would somehow cause recourse in my job that I worked so hard to do well. And I did do well. A range of promotions and success were the backbone of me thinking I was normal and perfectly functioning.

I called my depression, when it got bad, 'the darkness'. I can only describe it was being in a blacked-out metal cell, emotionally cold and alone, within a larger stone room. There was no way out once you were inside and the worst bit was when you could sense when it was coming. I used to get really upset when the onset started because I didn't want it coming back. In this room was a tiny piece of light that I couldn't reach – and through that was the World around me. I could see it – my friends, loved ones, colleagues, even later my own children – but I wasn't totally there and was always out of reach. There were times that I wanted it all to end again – but after having three wonderful children I knew that it wasn't an option. So I battled on.

Twenty years after the abuse started, and during the therapy, I was diagnosed with complex PTSD (Post Traumatic Stress Disorder) caused by trauma of being controlled and abused in the marriage. I will always remember that day; I wasn't mad, I wasn't depressed and it could have happened to anyone. It wasn't my fault.

I didn't want to seek help initially but accepting it changed my life. I opened up to those around me to an extent, still now living with a fear of stigma and them seeing me differently, but it is enough for me – I got help and that is important. I initially tried to open up to my sisters, but I then started to see the horror on their faces and quickly changed track, even joking about it. I would say to anyone trying to battle depressive or dissociative symptoms on their own to seek help – it will not go away on its own.

Professionally I now feel sharper – every day was a battle to connect with people and to seem 'normal'. Regulating my emotions, especially with my position was tough and a bigger struggle than helping to lead a school. I also used to overthink things. Now I feel that nearly anything can be achieved – my energy levels are higher and I have also realised the importance of exercise – it does help!

My experience has taught me the importance of education. I am lucky to have numerous qualifications that held me in good stead throughout my life and opened many doors. However, it wasn't the qualification that saved me. It was a friendship – the importance of which can never be underestimated or cherished enough.

Children need to feel safe and be equipped with social and emotional skills in order to thrive in the real world. Because of this, education is now so much more than gaining the 'expected' standard – don't get me wrong – it is important to open doors and to get the jobs they want and thus raising wellbeing and sense of achievement. Great education should result academic success coupled with an intrinsic knowledge of self and being successful as a whole person. That is the agenda that schools should now face. That is what will truly create the difference we all strive to make on a daily basis.

Important things I learnt that fellow teachers may benefit from:

- If you do feel depressed see a professional to talk to on a regular basis – make sure they are qualified.

- If it is affecting your role, or you feel that it could be, then seek help.

- Do not share all your problems with everyone. Be discreet and choose key, trusted people.

- Medication can help in the short term – they may cause side-affects so a half term is best to start these if you can wait.

- Keep busy – it is so easy to shut people out – that is the opposite to what you need to be doing.

- If you have a good relationship with your head teacher, then be open and honest about the condition.

- Exercise is great – get to a gym and stick to your timetable.

- Eat healthily – I binged a lot and it made me feel worse!

- Get a good amount of sleep – aim for at least 8 hours.

- Practice mindfulness and being at peace within yourself.

- Make sure your partner also gets support – it will also be difficult for them when trying to support you.

'You can be the cleverest kid in the world but you won't get anywhere if you can't have a conversation. For people like me a social and emotional education is so much more valuable than an academic one.' – Luke Dicker, a young man on the autism spectrum

CHAPTER 14
Talk to the Professionals –
Shaping the curriculum

Ilse Fullarton

The Children's Health Project is a Community Interest Company founded by Ilse Fullarton, a teacher and Physical Education Specialist in Primary Education, Personal Trainer and Nutrition Coach.

Four steps to a fresh health and wellbeing curriculum

Within the last three years, my conversations about 'health and wellbeing' with primary aged children have included:

- A five-year-old telling me they need 'whiter teeth'.
- Two seven-year-olds explaining their understanding of 'health' as 'counting calories' and 'looking good in a bikini'.

- A nine-year-old finishing the sentence 'when I feel healthy, I...' with 'look nice and slim' and 'when I feel unhealthy, I...' with 'look like a fatty'.
- An 11-year-old saying that healthy bodies are 'skinny and strong'.

These concerns seem confused and alarming to me. They shine a light on 'health' as it is portrayed in the media (mainly social media) – as strongly linked to appearance and weight. Both of which form the basis of many mental and social health issues in adults I have worked with over the last few years. In order for us to ensure our pupils are growing up strong, confident and able to make informed health decisions, our only option is to listen, and tackle these misrepresentations through our education system, at school – the heart of our community, where families feel supported by professionals.

I believe our education system is struggling to help children deeply understand health and wellbeing as a holistic topic, one that can give them tools to flourish and thrive in our modern world. We do a lot of PE, and teachers have worked hard to raise participation and enthuse children about movement. We cook with children and teach them about where foods come from, how to grow them, and teach balanced diets. We communicate the concerns about sugar, and previously foods high in fat. We hold circle time and deal with issues that arise on the playground. Teachers are doing so much for Health and Wellbeing in schools. Yet still we continue to see disturbing research on children's physical and mental health.

Over the last year, the following sentiments have been collected from children aged 4-11 years, from schools that are part of our project, when describing what they know about health and wellbeing:

Exercise is good for us

Sport is fun!

It feels good to run, jump, swim, etc.

Fruit and vegetables are good for us

Junk food is unhealthy

We should eat vitamins

It's bad to eat sugar

We shouldn't eat too many calories

We use sunscreen so we don't burn

It's healthy to be outside

We should drink lots of water

We should brush our teeth

We shouldn't stay on our tablets for too long

It feels good to relax

It's important to sleep

It's nice to feel calm

We should be kind to other people

Our brains have to be calm so we can think

We want to feel happy

We must not be violent

It's important to make good choices

We shouldn't worry so much

Yet still, when I ask them 'why?' the most common answer circles back round to 'because it's good for you', hinting that our pupils have little depth of knowledge when it comes to their own health. How are we expecting them to make healthy choices, and commit to healthy lifestyles, if they are simply learning a set of rules that even most adults struggle to relate to? It's only when we fully engage in a sense of vitality, of thriving as our best selves, that we find a commitment to taking care of ourselves. We currently have a prime opportunity to deeply nourish our pupils with information, wonder and experiences to enrich their understanding of health for their bodies and minds. We can help children flourish, and thrive, as opposed to survive.

Our vision is for all children to have greater respect for their bodies, have the knowledge and confidence to make sustainable healthy choices, and have a true understanding of why it is important to be healthy. We aim to make a sustainable change in health education, with an emphasis on cross-curricular teaching in PE, science and PSHE, and offer real-life support for parents and families. We offer a cross-curricular approach to Health and Wellbeing in EYFS, Key Stage 1 and Key Stage 2, combining movement, nutrition, lifestyle and mindset education in schools and online. We work with children (both within school and online), their teachers, and their families. We have created an effective system that allows schools to connect their good practice across the National Curriculum to identify a clear health and wellbeing curriculum, and initiate daily discussion about their bodies and minds to give them a fighting chance at making the healthiest choices they possibly can. The following steps may support your school to do the same, creating a holistic, relevant and sustainable health and wellbeing curriculum for your pupils.

Step 1: Identify your school's main health concerns
Asking (all) staff members whether children in your school are healthy/ unhealthy, reinforced by their own anecdotal evidence allows you to form an understanding of health issues your school could tackle through a health and wellbeing curriculum. Use the four topic areas of Healthy Movement, Healthy Eating, Healthy Habits and Healthy Thoughts to guide their responses. Combine this with evidence from surveys such as the SHEU survey, any Healthy Schools research and local evidence to create a picture of health issues that require attention in your school.

During a staff meeting, gather the evidence, and identify key topics for concern. Following this, look at your PE, science, DT and PSHE curricular to establish whether any of these issues are already being tackled across these subjects. Do the teachers feel learning in these subjects is relevant, has depth and breadth? Are there any cross-curricular approaches between these subjects? Do they link to your Healthy Schools ambitions? Does the school utilise funding to tackle these anecdotal issues?

Step 2: Create a system that communicates health and wellbeing concepts
Primary teaching has a secret power: themes/topics. We communicate knowledge and develop understanding by helping children to make links across several subjects, in a variety of environments, and in relevant contexts. They enable us to foster a love of learning, and for children to learn about a topic, in a memorable and engaging manner. For this reason, The Children's Health Project developed four key areas of learning, which organises much of our 'health education' (currently taught through PE, science, DT and PSHE) into a system, which is easily communicated to the children, staff and parents.

When a school becomes part of the Children's Health Project, they choose to teach a health and wellbeing programme centred around 12 learning outcomes for the whole school. These could also be used in your school, for a holistic approach, or you can develop your own with your staff:

Healthy movement
Everyone wishes to live a long life, full of adventure and activity. Truly valuing our amazing bodies, not for how they look, but for the incredible things they are capable of, brings pleasure to this adventure and activity. Someone who cherishes their physical health will have a deep understanding of how their body works. They will listen to their body, respond to how it feels, and learn from their daily movements. In respecting their body like this, they will develop a confidence to try new things, a commitment to self-care, and a competence to master any movement they choose. Providing all children (of any age) with the opportunity to play and explore, lays the foundation for this life of adventure. Building on their love of movement, with specific teaching of basic skills, in a variety of environments, develops confidence in their body's abilities. Fostering a love of movement, and a respect for their abilities, drives them to learn more about their bodies.

Learning outcomes:

- Pupils demonstrate motivation and confidence to engage in daily physical activity.

- Pupils are moving for at least one hour a day (moderate to vigorous activity).

- Pupils feel knowledgeable about their body.

Healthy eating
A nourished body feeds achievement, attainment, satisfaction and happiness. Unfortunately, in our modern world of convenience and immediacy, many

have lost sight of some basic human needs, and it's having catastrophic consequences. Children of primary age know no different. They are dependent on adults feeding them well, and trust their carers. Yet if the carers themselves are dependent on the information from the food industry, and innocently trust the products sold to them, the fundamental knowledge and understanding of how to nourish a body can become lost. If we can supplement their nourishing diets with deep learning, of which foods and drinks will fulfil their needs, why they are good for them and how they will impact their bodies, children are more likely to develop a healthy relationship with food, and make healthy choices that fuel their adventurous lifestyles.

Learning outcomes:

- Pupils demonstrate an awareness of healthy and less healthy foods.
- Pupils make healthy food choices most of the time.
- Pupils demonstrate an understanding of how food affects their body, in terms of mood, energy and immunity.

Healthy habits

To thrive with a healthy lifestyle, we need to adopt daily healthy habits. Many see these habits as the thread that runs through an overall sense of wellbeing. We have been taught from an early age that these habits will impact our zest for life – sleep, hydration, fresh air, laughter – all should play a part in our recipe for a long, fulfilling life. For children, health becomes achievable and less daunting with simple daily habits, and these lifestyle choices may form the key to complete wellbeing. By combining habits such as hobbies, routine, laughter, moderation and abundance with healthy eating, movement and thoughts, we create a health ecology so strong, our children could flourish, despite modern health disruptors. Healthy habits encourage more interaction with the natural environment; it gives children an opportunity to reflect on their daily actions, and the tools to upgrade their health and wellbeing.

Learning outcomes:

- Pupils have a range of tools to improve their health through daily habits such as sleep, hydration, breathing techniques and dental health.
- Pupils show an awareness of their feelings, and have strategies to deal with emotional difficulties.

Healthy thoughts

As teachers, we are striving for the best for our pupils, desperately juggling the need for them to achieve in all curriculum areas, but also to feel excited by learning, and the journey of life they have just begun. Mental and emotional wellbeing stands out as the driving force behind attainment and achievement: learners cannot achieve their best without feeling their best. In our busy, stressful world, we should be teaching our pupils to find enjoyment in drive and ambition, joy in success, and resilience in challenge. If they can develop strategies to plan an exciting future, work towards it by learning new skills, learn from their mistakes and any barriers they are faced with, success will seem much sweeter when it's achieved. Understanding how their body and mind works, and how they can utilise essential skills in mindset is the key to unlock this happiness.

Learning outcomes:

- Pupils demonstrate a positive body image.
- Pupils show an awareness of mindfulness, and endeavour to be mindful in their daily lives.
- Pupils exude positivity and motivation.
- Pupils develop resilient attitudes and are tolerant of others.

Step 3: Teach health and wellbeing with positive role models

Each school needs role models to communicate the new Health and Wellbeing system. A fundamental part of the project's success has been our Health Champions. They guide the children through the curriculum; inspire them with daily interaction, and act as role models to children who struggle to name a 'healthy person' in their lives. Younger pupils respond particularly well to characters like this; older pupils use the characters as a reminder of the system, and when collaborating, guide younger pupils with examples from the Health Champions. The Health Champions feature in our schools' assemblies, lessons, playgrounds, newsletters, brochures, foyers and letters. They communicate the system of learning we wish the children to remember and utilise to make healthy choices.

Captain Kinetic© represents healthy movement

Captain Kinetic is inquisitive in play, confident in daily movement and ambitious when challenged. Having developed a wide range of movement skills, he strives for success in all arenas, yet is resilient to defeat with his supple attitude. He's a brave competitor, who admires his rivals and challenges with a smile. He sees varied terrain as an opportunity to climb and scramble, trusting his body to support his appetite for adventure. A role model to others, he uplifts his team. Balancing sport with creativity, he enjoys a range of activities, and never says no to a new challenge. He goes to sleep naturally exhausted, enthusiastic to traverse tomorrow's encounters.

Nutrition Ninja represents healthy eating©

Nutrition Ninja searches the world for her favourite recipes, savouring every delicious flavour, and feeling safe in the knowledge that her food is fuelling her adventurous life, her healthy body and her mind. She realises the power of food, not only for taste, but also to nourish her body and brain, both working hard everyday. With her knowledge and understanding of nutrients, she can select foods to support her needs, nurturing her great moods and steady energy levels. Food and drink are powerhouses of goodness for Nutrition Ninja, who cares about and respects their origins and carefully considers her diverse diet to make her feel vibrant!

Agent Lifestyle© represents healthy habits

Agent Lifestyle places in value in some of the forgotten health secrets of past. He sleeps deeply for long periods, resting his mind and body to prepare for new learning. Every cell in his active, nourished body is plump with water, bringing clarity to challenging tasks. Outside, he breathes the fresh air that will aid his sleep, while the

sun shines on as much of his skin as possible, allowing his body to produce Vitamin D for his bones and immunity. He fills his days with healthy hobbies, whilst maintaining balance with routine. Generally, his life is experienced in moderation, but abundance blossoms with healthy foods and activities. When spending time with family and friends, his teeth glisten with a happy smile.

Mindset Warrior© represents healthy thoughts

Mindset Warrior is at peace with herself. She sets goals, works towards them, picks herself up when she falls, and considers other people in her actions. She values herself – not for her appearance, but for her zest for life and the enjoyment she finds in interactions with people and the world around her. She strives to achieve, but not necessarily for perfection. She senses the good in others and works on self-development in order to feel a sense of fulfilment. A warrior instead of a worrier, she demonstrates resilience and kindness, both to herself and others.

Step 4: Immerse the children in rich learning

Schools within our project find most success when they take steps to embed change and ensure it is community wide. Considering all learners – teachers, pupils and parents is crucial in ensuring behaviour change. We don't only train teachers to understand and deliver the programme; we also run children's workshops – half-day experiences to immerse the children in learning about health and wellbeing under the four key areas of learning. Launching your new health and wellbeing curriculum could include some exciting themed days, where you invite members of the health community in to inspire the children. Furthermore, schools within our Project feel the link to parents and families is strengthened with workshops where parents can learn about foods, activities and discuss body image issues and how to speak to their children about the stresses of modern life. Could your school hold a support group for parents and families, either by inviting all to join, or targeting parents you feel need additional help? Pockets of funding are available to accommodate these needs, and should be utilised to meet your school's bespoke priorities. Appointing members of staff to oversee specific aspects of your health and wellbeing curriculum allows for a balanced approach. If curriculum lessons can be enriched with extra curricular activities, such as a health club of sorts, any sports/movement clubs, cookery club, and mindful activities (such as board games, sewing, knitting, gardening, beekeeping etc.), your school will be providing a broad, rich learning environment where children feel informed and supported to make healthy choices.

If you or your school adopts any of these steps, please get in touch and tell us about your success. We love to hear of schools that develop their own health and wellbeing approach.

admin@childrenshealthproject.com

'You can drag my body to school but my spirit refuses to go.' –
Bill Watterson, The Essential Calvin and Hobbes

CHAPTER 15

Talk to the Professionals – Not working for a significant minority: A critical exploration of SEND and SEMH in the context of schools

Jon Reid, Brookes University

Introduction

Developing an understanding of a broad range of Special Educational Needs and Disabilities (SEND) is challenging.

Appreciating the relationship between SEND and Social, Emotional and Mental Health (SEMH) can be difficult.

Recognising the co-interaction of SEND and SEMH in the context of schools adds an additional layer of complexity.

This chapter aims to provide a brief exploration of important considerations with regards to SEND and SEMH. A reflection on personal experiences of working with children and young people (CYP) with SEMH needs is followed by an overview of current concerns with regards to the Educational experiences of children with SEMH needs who may be 'vulnerable', 'marginalised' and 'excluded'. These concerns are then discussed in relation to the influence of policy on practice. Previous attempts at 'defining' and 'categorising' this group of CYP are then critiqued before introducing the concept of complexity with regards to understanding SEMH needs in the specific context of schools. The chapter concludes by encouraging careful consideration of 'what works' in terms of 'evidence-based' approaches to supporting CYP with SEMH needs in our schools.

The importance of personal experiences and reflection when understanding SEMH needs

I have been very fortunate to have worked in a variety of educational settings throughout my teaching career and recognise that such experiences have and will continue to influence my understanding of CYP who experience SEMH needs and my responses to behaviours that may challenge in the specific context of schools.

Having initially worked in a mainstream primary school, I became passionate about supporting CYP with additional learning needs and particularly those who, like me, were, at times, disinterested, disaffected and disengaged in education.

These early teaching experiences inspired me to actively pursue opportunities to explore why current Educational approaches are not working for a significant minority of CYP in the UK who exhibit SEMH needs and are 'vulnerable', 'marginalised' and 'excluded' both within and from a wide range of education settings and provisions.

Teaching in a prodigious residential school provided powerful insights into therapeutic ways of understanding and working with severely traumatised primary aged children (The Mulberry Bush School, 2017). Such insights informed, and continue to influence my approaches to supporting all CYP but particularly those who have experienced adverse childhood experiences (WHO, 2017).

My then role as a local authority behaviour support teacher, when such roles still existed, provided opportunities to work with senior leadership colleagues, SENCOs, teachers and pupils in early years, primary and secondary settings, their parents/carers and a wide range of professionals. This role provided useful insights into the importance of working together to develop shared understandings of difficulties experienced and behaviours exhibited in specific contexts through collaborating to strategically plan individualised approaches with the aim of improving educational experiences.

Prior to my current role, I was appointed as a deputy headteacher to support the development of a new Independent SEMH secondary special school for permanently excluded children and young people who exhibited complex learning needs, communication difficulties and challenging behaviours. These children and young people had experienced multiple school moves and exclusions, spent time in pupil referral units, local authority special schools, being home schooled with limited opportunities for learning or social interaction or attended a variety of alternative provisions. The headteacher, an inspirational and experienced colleague who had spent his entire career working with children and young people who may challenge, often reminded me that it's not the children that have failed schools, it is the schools that have failed the children.

As a school community, we recognised our role in creating opportunities for pupils to frequently experience success and positive recognition for their achievements socially, emotionally and academically through adapting our pedagogy and practice, differentiating our approaches to discipline and developing genuine, unconditional positive relationships to encourage feelings of belonging, emotional security, enjoyment of learning and, we hoped, re-engagement in education.

In my current role, at a higher education institution, I now enjoy opportunities to work with a wide range of practitioners, professionals, academics, undergraduate and postgraduate students who share my interest in trying to understand more about the Educational experiences of these 'vulnerable', 'marginalised' and 'excluded' CYP.

This role enables me to engage in ongoing, critical explorations of theoretical ideas, policy and practice in relation to understanding the complexity of SEMH needs in our schools.

My experiences and engagement with research to date continues to confirm my recognition that understanding, interpreting, responding and supporting the social, emotional and mental health needs of all children and young people and particularly those with additional needs, involves an appreciation of a broad range of inter-disciplinary and, often alternative, sociological, historical, philosophical and psychological perspectives.

Contextualising concerns about SEMH needs
The World Health Organisation (WHO) recognises that, internationally, 1 in 5 (or 20%) children experience a mental health condition and that 'the impact of unaddressed child and adolescent mental health conditions is large scale and long-term' (WHO, 2010, p.20). For children and young people experiencing

social, emotional and mental health needs, these 'can be both a cause and a consequence of the experience of social, civil, political, economic, and environmental inequalities' (WHO, 2010, p. 29).

In the UK, it has been reported that 'children and young people with poor mental health are more likely to have poor educational attainment and employment prospects, social relationship difficulties, physical ill health and substance misuse problems and to become involved in offending' (Davis, 2014, p. 101).

While current policy guidance recognises that 'one in ten children and young people aged 5 to 16 has a clinically diagnosed mental health disorder and around one in seven has less severe problems' (DfE, 2016, p. 4), it is important to appreciate that for some populations of CYP these figures are likely to be much higher. While exploring the prevalence of SEMH needs in special school populations, Hackett, Theodosiou, Bond, Blackburn, Spicer and Lever, for example, found that '95.7% of the young people scored in the abnormal range on the summative scores on the four subdivisions of hyperkinesis, conduct disorders, peer problems and emotional disorders' (2010, p. 151). Indeed, in my pervious special school, 100% of the CYP attending that provision exhibited a broad range of complex and often overlapping, co-morbid, SEMH needs that were reflected in their education, health and care plans.

For CYP with SEND – particularly those with complex learning difficulties – it is, therefore, important to appreciate that 'mental health is the most pervasive and co-occurring need to compound and complicate children's special educational needs and disabilities' (Carpenter and Egerton, 2011, p. 24).

Additionally, it is recognised by Bernard and Turk (2009, p. 1) that 'children and adolescents with developmental disabilities are at a greater risk of developing mental health or behavioural problems than are their nondisabled peers'.

Special educational needs and disabilities are, therefore, considered to be one of many 'risk factors' in developing SEMH needs throughout childhood and adolescence.

These risks increase and have a multiplicative effect if a child or young person is exposed to more than one risk. Such risks have been identified as 'social disadvantage, family adversity and cognitive or attention problems' by Brown, Khan & Parsonage (2012, p. 18).

Additionally, Kendall, Straw, Jones, Springate and Grayson (2008, p. 22) state that vulnerable groups of children and young people also include 'children with disabilities, children looked after, children with behaviour problems, antisocial behaviour and conduct disorders and children at risk of committing crime'.

The National Foundation for Educational Research (NFER, 2017) includes a broad range of categories of CYP who may be vulnerable, disengaged and disadvantaged with regards to educational achievement, attainment, attendance and exclusion, all of which can contribute to the development of SEMH needs. The current 'Mental Health and Behaviour in Schools' policy (DfE, 2016) provides useful guidance and more detail with regards to potential risks that may contribute to the development of SEMH needs. Here 'risks' that relate to the CYP themselves, their families, communities or experiences of difficult life events are described in addition to 'protective characteristics' that 'enable children to be resilient when they encounter problems and challenges' (DfE, 2016, p. 8-10).

SEMH tensions: policy, teacher responsibilities and concerns

Schools and therefore teachers 'are increasingly seen as a key focus for future work for mental health promotion and intervention' (Davies, 2014, p. 104). Indeed, statutory guidance with regards to SEMH included in the Special Educational Needs and Disability Code of Practice: 0 to 25 years states that:

'Schools and colleges should have clear processes to support children and young people, including how they will manage the effect of any disruptive behaviour so it does not adversely affect other pupils' (DfE/DoH, 2015, p. 98).

Additionally, while mental health and behaviour in schools recognises that 'only medical professionals should make a formal diagnosis of a mental health condition', it is also stated that schools, 'are well-placed to observe children day-to-day and identify those whose behaviour suggests that they may be suffering from a mental health problem or be at risk of developing one' (DfE, 2016, p. 14).

In recognition of the complexity of SEMH, previous research has indicated that 'teachers and other professional colleagues often feel ill-prepared to address mental health difficulties experienced by their pupils' (Rose, Howley, Fergusson and Jament, 2009, p. 3). Indeed, more recently, despite 91% of school staff surveyed suggesting that they know of pupils experiencing anxiety or panic attacks, 79% depression, 64% self-harm, 49% eating disorders and 47% OCD, both senior leaders and classroom teachers raised concerns about:

- Feeling equipped to identify behaviour that may be linked to a mental health issue.
- Being equipped to teach children in their classes who have mental health needs.
- Knowing how to help students with mental health issues access support offered within school (Smith, Tattersall, Rabiasz and Sims, 2017).

Additional tensions evident in current policy documentation relate to how we as teachers understand, interpret and respond to behaviours of concern in schools.

While the SEND Code of Practice recognises 'withdrawn or isolated, as well as displaying challenging, disruptive or disturbing behaviour' (DoH/DfE, 2015, p. 98) as indicators of social and emotional 'difficulties' that might be associated with an unmet SEMH need, behaviour and discipline in schools provides guidance with regards to schools statutory responsibilities and teachers 'powers' to discipline 'pupils whose behaviour is unacceptable, who break the school rules or who fail to follow a reasonable instruction' (DfE, 2016a, p. 6).

Constructions and re-conceptualisations of SEMH

How we construct and conceptualise the behaviour of CYP with regards to SEMH needs influences our understanding of such behaviour in context, our active interpretation of reasons for those behaviours and our subsequent responses and implementation of appropriate strategies for support. Despite a fall in the number of children and young people being excluded from schools over the last ten years or so, it is concerning to note an increase in both fixed term and permanent exclusions across all age groups and all school types more recently (DfE, 2017).

Concerns have been raised both internationally (Johnson, 2016, Korpershoek, Harms, de Boer, van Kuijk, Doolaard, 2016, Slee, 2015, and here in the UK (McAllister, 2014, Oxley, 2015, Sullivan, 2016, Weare, 2015) with regards the characteristics of excluded pupils (DfE, 2012) and the over-representation of specific groups of children and young people in these exclusion statistics such as those with SEMH needs and additional vulnerabilities that may relate to their experiences of multiple risk factors in their daily lives.

Such concerns have been expressed in relation to the current responses to behaviours of concern recommended in policy documentation that involve consequences, sanctions and punishments (e.g. DfE, 2016a). Such concerns recognise recent research that identified a bi-directional relationship between SEMH needs and exclusions.

As part of a study exploring the impact of being excluded from school in relation to measures of psychological distress (Ford, Parker, Salim, Goodman, Henley, 2017) it was found that:

'Excluded children can develop a range of mental disorders, such as depression and anxiety as well as behavioural disturbance. The impact of excluding a child from school on their education and progress is often long term, and this work suggests that their mental health may also deteriorate' (Ford, 2017).

It is therefore important to recognise such concerns and to appreciate that 'there are alternatives to the behaviourist DfE rhetoric and these alternatives take into consideration the social, emotional and attachment needs of the children in your classroom' (Reid, 2017, p. 249).

To be able to critically interpret the current context of SEMH in schools, it is important to appreciate how previous explorations, considerations and understandings have influenced how this group of children and young people have been described and therefore represented in policy historically.

Jones reminds us that terminology used to categorise children who may engage in behaviours that challenge has changed over time. Such changes have then been reflected in policy and influenced how schools and therefore teachers respond to such behaviour. Jones describes changes in categorisation from:

Maladjusted
Where disruptive behaviour was understood, prior to 1981 Education Act, as a function of psychopathology and was, therefore, understood from a 'medical' perspective that required 'treatment' in a specific environment such as a special school.

Emotional and Behavioural Difficulties (EBD)
Influenced by social and behavioural sciences, developmental and eco-systemic approaches, 'disorderly behaviour or disaffection' was then re-defined as a special educational need resulting from emotional and behavioural difficulties. Practical responses to behaviours of concern would then ideally be supported in mainstream schools, with opportunities for excluded pupils to attend pupil referral units as a type of 'rehabilitation' facility.

This shift reconceptualised challenging behaviour in terms of the need for an educational response (Jones, 2003).

In the previous SEN Code of Practice (DfES, 2001), some children were categorised as experiencing 'Behaviour, Emotion and Social Development' difficulties (BESD), also referred to in literature as 'Social, Emotional and Behavioural Development' difficulties' (SEBD).

However, these children and young people are now identified as having SEMH needs (DfE/DoH, 2015).

From this brief synopsis of changing conceptualisations and subsequent categorisations of behaviours that may challenge and the mental health of CYP in policy, it is clear that: 'teachers' responses to problems in the classroom are staged against social representations of difficult behaviour, which in turn are formed against the backdrop of educational goals' (Jones, 2003, p.151).

SEND, SEMH & complexity

The current SEND Code of Practice recognises the following broad range of 'mental health difficulties':

- Anxiety or depression.
- Self-harming.
- Substance misuse.
- Eating disorders or physical symptoms that are medically unexplained.
- Disorders such as: Attention Deficit Disorder, Attention Deficit Hyperactive Disorder or Attachment Disorder (DoH/DfE, 2015, p. 97).

However, as discussed previously, it is important to recognise that some children and young people may meet more than one criteria (co-morbidity) within the Code of Practice 'for instance speech, language and communication needs can also be a feature of a number of other areas of SEN, and children with an Autism Spectrum Disorder may have needs across all areas' and that individual needs will change over time (DoH/DfE, 2015, p. 85).

SEMH as a category of SEND is therefore complex and requires inter-disciplinary understandings. To address recent concerns about appropriate interpretations of behaviours may challenge and responses to associated SEMH needs, it is useful to consider a broad range of theoretical conceptualisations that offer alternative perspectives when considering the various ways to support children and young people who exhibit SEMH needs in our schools.

Such theoretical conceptualisations have been explored in detail elsewhere however Hart provides a useful summary with regards to:

Behavioural approaches

Which offer a reductionist, oversimplified understanding of the nature and causes of behaviour through the use of rewards and punishment.

Psychodynamic approaches

Which promote the importance of nurturing stable, caring and trusting relationships by drawing on Attachment theories.

Systemic approaches

Which recognise the influence of complex interactions between individuals, families, schools, communities and wider society where 'no blame' cultures encourage collaboration to respond appropriately to any concerns about behaviour.

Humanistic approaches

Which encourage positive teacher-pupil relationships through exhibiting empathy, genuine, unconditional positive regard, non-directivity, autonomy and choice in learning to develop self-esteem, identity and efficacy, rather than oppression and control (2010, p. 356-359).

Additionally, Cooper offers an influential philosophical critique of our understanding SEMH needs through his exploration of ADHD in the context of schools from a bio-psychosocial perspective (2008). This bio-psychosocial perspective can also be usefully applied to other neurological conditions such as Autism, Foetal Alcohol Spectrum Disorder, Tourette's or Attachment Disorders, for example.

Although prevalence rates differ globally, in the UK ADHD is thought to affect about 3-9% of school age CYP and is associated with symptoms of hyperactivity/impulsivity and/or inattention (NICE, 2017).

Cooper suggests that understanding ADHD requires recognition of three main theoretical influences, cognitive psychology, neurobiological research and genetic research (2008).

From a cognitive psychology perspective, children and young people with ADHD are known to experience difficulties in relation to self-regulation, impulsiveness, and executive functioning, specifically in relation to working memory, which influences the ability to inhibit or delay behavioural responses and the retention of information for future planning.

Recent studies have found that these cognitive functions are related to neurophysiological mechanisms, such as those associated with the frontal lobes of the brain and neurobiological influences such as specific neurotransmitter systems. The influence of these neurobiological factors on cognitive functioning, particularly in relation to the neurotransmitter Dopamine, has been supported by genetic research with monozygotic (identical) and dizygotic (non-identical) twin studies where there is a greater incidence of ADHD in monozygotic twins (Cooper, 2008).

However, it is also important to recognise that 'environmental' or social influences have been implicated in the development of ADHD. Such influences are summarised by Cooper as being parenting skills, disorderly home environments, marital discord between parents, maternal mental health and paternal personality factors.

For Cooper, ADHD is therefore 'a behavioural manifestation with its origins in a biologically-based pre-disposition' (2008, p. 461). As ADHD is influenced by biological and social factors, society then 'socially constructs' our understanding of children and young people who are diagnosed with ADHD as being 'disordered' arguing that:

'The school is a major setting where this process of social construction takes place, and it is through the patterns of institutional control and pedagogical practices that such construction is implemented' (Cooper, 2008, p. 461).

The need for those working in education to consider a broad range of theoretical perspectives to understand the reasons for behaviours that challenge in schools in a specific context, at specific times, which do not rely in cohesion, control and punishment has been proposed by Slee (2010) who recognises that:

'Understanding structural and individual underpinnings supports more nuanced responses to the interactions of students and teachers mediated through pedagogy, curriculum, the processes of schooling, the dynamics of classroom organisation and culture' (2015, p. 8).

'Evidence-based' approaches, SEND and SEMH

Current rhetoric relating to Education policy and practice is concerned with 'evidence-based' approaches and the implementation of 'what works' to support children and young people with regards to their school experiences and learning. It is hoped that the exploration for SEND and SEMH here reveals challenges to the application of 'what works' with regards to the behaviour of some young children and young people in our schools. Despite clear recognition that that responses to behaviour that rely on sanctions, consequences and punishments are ineffective, current policy continues to focus on and promote "authoritarian approaches to discipline and disruptive behaviour" (Ford *et al,* 2017 n.p).

As has been advocated throughout this chapter, we, as teachers, have a responsibility to carefully consider the reasons for behaviour that may challenge. The complexity of behaviour from the perspective of SEND and SEMH requires an appreciation of potential 'vulnerability', 'marginalisation' and 'exclusion' from Education. While considering behaviour from a biopsychosocial perspective is useful and encourages reflection on the influence of school-based decision making, this perspective must be considered in relation to broader societal and policy influences on practice.

To be able to effectively support children and young people who may engage in behaviours that challenge, the reconceptualisation, categorisation and construction of our understanding from difficult, challenging, and disordered to those with SEMH needs is important.

According to Professor Barry Carpenter:

'What we see in this new generation of children with complex learning needs is vulnerability, particularly in the emotional development. Vulnerable learners are fragile learners, and our quest as educators has to be 'how do we make our children emotionally strong?' (2017, p. 9)

Alternative approaches to understanding and responding to behaviours that may challenge at whole school, small group and individual levels are those that focus on the social and emotional development of our children and young people. Approaches that are founded on an appreciation of social and emotional development, attachment theories (Colley and Cooper, 2017) and the importance of compassion and positive relationships will help ensure 'that the children in your class will experience empowerment, recognition, respect and most importantly, feelings of connectedness and belonging' (Reid, 2017, p. 261).

References

Bernard, S. and Turk, J. (2009): Developing Mental Health Services for Children and Adolescents with Learning Disabilities: A Toolkit for Clinicians. London: RCPsych Publications in collaboration with the National CAMHS Support Service.

Brown, E., Khan, L. and Parsonag, M. (2012): A chance to change: Delivering effective parenting programmes to transform lives. London: Centre for Mental Health.

Carpenter, B. (2017): Foreword in Colley & Cooper (Eds). *Emotional Development and Attachment in the Classroom: Theory and Practice for Students and Teachers*. London: Jessica Kingsley Publishers.

Carpenter, B. and Egerton, J. (2011): The Complex Learning Difficulties and Disabilities Research Project: Developing meaningful pathways to personalised learning. London: Specialist Schools and Academies Trust.

Cooper, P. (2010): Like Alligators Bobbing for Poodles? A Critical Discussion of Education, ADHD and the Bio-psychosocial Perspective. Wiley-Blackwell: *Journal of Philosophy of Education*. Vol. 42, no. 3-4, p. 457-474.

Colley, D. and Cooper, P. (2017): *Emotional Development and Attachment in the Classroom: Theory and Practice for Students and Teachers*. London: Jessica Kingsley Publishers.

Davies, S. (2014): Annual Report of the Chief Medical Officer 2013. Public Mental Health Priorities: Investing in the Evidence. London: Department of Health.

Department for Education (2012): Ensuring good behaviour in schools. A summary for headteachers, governing bodies, teachers, parents and pupils. London: Department for Education.

Department for Education (2016): Mental Health and Behaviour in Schools. London: Department for Education.

Department for Education (2016a): Behaviour and discipline in schools: Advice for headteachers and school staff. London: Department for Education.

Department for Education (2017): Permanent and fixed-period exclusions in England: 2015 to 2016. London: Department for Education.

Department for Education/Department of Health (2015): Special educational needs and disability code of practice: 0 to 25 years: Statutory guidance for organisations which work with and support children and young people who have special educational needs or disabilities. London: Department for Education.

Department for Education and Skills (2001): Special Educational Needs Code of Practice. London: Department for Education.

Ford, T. (2017): Exclusion from school can trigger long-term psychiatric illness. University of Exeter: Featured News. Available at: www.exeter.ac.uk/news/featurednews/title_595920_en.html (Accessed: 27/11/2017).

Ford, T., Parker, C., Salim, J, Goodman, R and Henley, W. (2017): The Relationship between Exclusion from School and Mental Health: A Secondary Analysis of The British Child and Adolescent Mental Health Surveys 2004 and 2007, Psychological Medicine. Available at: www.exeter.ac.uk/media/universityofexeter/newsarchive/researchmedical/Psychological_Medicine_preprint1.pdf (Accessed: 27/11/2017).

Hackett, L, Theodosiou, L., Bond, C., Blackburn, C., Spicer, F. and Lever, R. (2010): Mental health needs in schools for emotional, behavioural and social difficulties. Wiley-Blackwell: *British Journal of Special Education*. Vol. 37, no. 3, p. 148-155.

Hart, R. (2010): Classroom behaviour management: Educational Psychologists' views on effective practice. *Emotional and Behavioural Difficulties*. Vol. 15, no. 4, p. 353-37.

Jones, R. (2003): The Construction of Emotional and Behavioural Difficulties. Routledge: *Educational Psychology in Practice*. Vol. 19, no. 2, p. 147-157.

Johnson, B. (2016): Daring to Disagree About School 'Discipline': An Australian Case Study of a Media-Led Backlash in Challenging Dominant Views on Student Behaviour at School Answering Back. Singapore: Springer. Vol. 1, p. 15-26.

Kendall, S., Straw, S., Jones, M., Springate, I. and Grayson, H. (2008): A Review of the Research Evidence: Narrowing the Gap in Outcomes for Vulnerable Groups. Slough: NFER.

Korpershoek, H., Harms, T., de Boer, H., van Kuijk, M. and Doolaard, S. (2016): A Meta-Analysis of the Effects of Classroom Management Strategies and Classroom Management Programs on Students' Academic, Behavioral, Emotional, and Motivational Outcomes. Sage Publications: *Review of Educational Research*, Vol. 86, no. 3, p. 643-680.

MacAllister, J. (2014): Why discipline needs to be reclaimed as an educational concept. Routledge: *Educational Studies*, Vol. 40, no. 4, p. 438-451.

NFER (2017): Vulnerable Groups. Slough: NFER. Available at: www.nfer.ac.uk/what-we-do/centre-for-policy-and-practice-research/vulnerable-groups/ (Accessed: 27/11/2017).

NICE (2017): Attention deficit hyperactivity disorder: diagnosis and management. London: NICE. Available at: www.nice.org.uk/guidance/cg72/chapter/Context (Accessed: 27/11/2017).

Oxley, L. (2015): Do schools need lessons on motivation? The British Psychological Society: *The Psychologist*, Vol. 29, no. 9, p. 722-772.

Reid, J. (2017): Emotional Development and approaches to Classroom Management. In Colley & Cooper (Eds). *Emotional Development and Attachment in the Classroom: Theory and Practice for Students and Teachers.* London: Jessica Kingsley Publishers.

Rose, R, Howley, M, Fergusson, A and Jament, J. (2009): Mental Health and SEN: Mental health and special educational needs: exploring a complex relationship. Wiley-Blackwell: *British Journal of Special Education*. Vol. 36, no. 1, p. 3-8.

Slee, R. (2015): Beyond a psychology of student behaviour. Taylor and Francis: *Emotional and Behavioural Difficulties*. Vol. 20, no. 1, p. 3-19.

Smith, R, Tattersall, J, Rabiasz, A and Sims, D. (2017): NFER Teacher Voice Omnibus: NFER Teacher Voice Omnibus: May to July 2016 survey. DfE Questions. London: Department for Education.

Sullivan, A. (2016): Schools' tough approach to bad behaviour isn't working – and may escalate problems. The Conversation. Available at: theconversation.com/schools-tough-approach-to-bad-behaviour-isnt-working-and-may-escalate-problems-56737

Weare, K. (2015): What works in promoting social and emotional wellbeing and responding to mental health problems in schools? Advice for Schools and Framework Document. London: National Children's Bureau. Partnership for Wellbeing and Mental Health in Schools.

WHO (2010): Mental Health and Development: Targeting people with mental health conditions as a vulnerable group. Geneva: The World Health Organisation.

WHO (2017): Adverse Childhood Experiences International Questionnaire (ACE-IQ). Available at: www.who.int/violence_injury_prevention/violence/activities/adverse_childhood_experiences/en/ (Accessed: 27/11/2017).

'And now that you don't have to be perfect, you can be good.' – John Steinbeck, East of Eden

CHAPTER 16
Talk to the Professionals –
Tackling educational disadvantage

Marc Rowland

Tackling educational disadvantage: A holistic approach

It is important for schools to focus on the building blocks, the processes for success for disadvantaged pupils. Too often (nationally), there is too great a focus on the 'outcome', leading to much energy and resources being targeted at Year 6 or 11. This leaves schools 'cohort vulnerable', particularly if evaluation is weak too.

The following ten measures can be used for schools to evaluate against. They are based on evidence from the most effective practice nationally. They should help ensure that no vulnerable learner slips through the tightening grip of our accountability system, which sometimes creates perverse incentives. They should help schools ascertain whether their strategies are sufficiently embedded. Pastoral and academic and strategies should be intertwined.

1. A school culture measure

Understanding the barriers to learning faced by vulnerable pupils is fundamental. This means recognising that barriers don't just sit with pupils themselves, but also within the community and within school. Have the in-school barriers to learning been recognised?

- Are attitudes to parents of vulnerable pupils positive? Is the language used to describe vulnerable pupils universally positive?
- Do teachers and support staff know their pupils, their interests? Do they support pupils in achieving the highest of ambitions?
- Is the Pupil Premium used to target high prior attaining pupils? Are pupils put in 'lower sets' based simply on Key Stage 2 SATs results? Do organisational needs take priority over the learner?
- What are the expectations of vulnerable pupils at the end of lessons, at the end of the day? How purposeful is learning in lower sets?
- What do pupils say about the relationships between adults and pupils?
- Be wary of meaningless and simplistic ability labels that are not supported by evidence.

2. An attainment measure

- All vulnerable pupils should be expected to make necessary progress to attain well in English and maths. Is attainment strong in subjects that will keep options and choices open?
- Do teachers and other staff believe that all pupils can attain well? Where attainment grouping is in place, is it based on evidence, where all pupils are expected to reach the same destinations and have the same expectations?
- Avoid only benchmarking internally. What does performance look like compared with the most effective schools nationally, using the Education Endowment Foundation's Families of School database?
- Visit those schools, even if, on the surface, their approach may different. What are the active ingredients for success in these schools?

3. A curriculum measure

- Do all pupils access knowledge rich-language rich curriculum that creates opportunity and choice? Avoid less rigorous learning opportunities for the sake of 'engagement'. Pupils who are not attaining well cannot catch up if they are provided with easier work. The best learning, the best engagement comes from rich cultural, technical and contextual knowledge. The most engaging and interesting learning is challenging.
- Are the opportunities to access this knowledge open to all, regardless of prior attainment?

- Where technical or vocational pathways are chosen, qualifications should be sufficiently robust to enable opportunity and choice if pupils change their minds?
- Are low prior attainers given access to a less rigorous curriculum?

4. An inclusion measure

- Do vulnerable pupils have access to high quality, well-trained, well-qualified staff at least in proportion to their peers? Are they able to frequently work alongside successful role models?
- Do vulnerable learners play a visible role in wider school life? Do they feel like they belong? Are their voices heard and do schools listen?
- Are the views of parents of vulnerable pupils actively heard and listened to?
- Are behaviour management systems based on evidence? Do they work? How do you know?
- Where pupils are removed from class for challenging behaviour, are they and their teachers still expected to work together to secure progress?

5. An oral language measure

- Oral language is a critical indicator for future attainment. Yet it rarely gets sufficient focus in secondary schools nationally. Is the curriculum language rich?
- Are classrooms language-rich? Is language development targeted sufficient at those who need it? Are there opportunities for pupils to think aloud together to develop collaborative lines of thinking?
- Are teachers sufficiently trained in SEMH to support vulnerable learners?
- Do these opportunities differ across classes (i.e. do 'lower' sets have fewer opportunities in order to manage behaviour)?
- Are pupils able to articulate their thinking clearly in spoken word? Do they have the subject-specific vocabulary to enable them to active participants in their learning?
- Are there clear strategies for teaching vocabulary? Just hearing it/ seeing it is not enough to embed. Being 'language rich' cannot be achieved through vocabulary being displayed and used in lessons. Are effective teaching strategies used to sufficiently impact on pupils?
- Is there sufficiently skilled speech therapy provision in school?

- Oral language and articulacy are fundamental to success beyond the classroom too. Are pupils given opportunities to practice these qualities?

6. A metacognitive measure

Poor dispositions towards learning and a lack of self-regulation strategies are frequently cited as a barrier to learning. These can sometimes be exaggerated by well-intentioned interventions in the name of 'support'. The best long-term, evidence-based strategy is to improve metacognition and self-regulation. Metacognition is part of excellent teaching and learning. It is the conscious application of learning strategies to enable pupils to overcome challenging tasks. It enables pupils to self-regulate and plan an approach to learning. Metacognition enables pupils to understand that learning does not happen by chance.

- Too many vulnerable pupils have not sufficiently developed metacognitive strategies, with teachers and leaders speaking of passive learners who lack independence. Is metacognition embedded within teaching and learning?

- This should ensure more accurate records of learning in books, enabling teachers to more effectively assess pupil progress. Correct answers in pupil's books are not necessarily a good proxy for learning if they have not had to think hard. Do books provide an accurate record of the process of learning?

- Are pupils able to articulate and explain what happens in the lessons where they learn the most?

7. An evidence measure

It is critical that school leaders do not cherry pick research that avoids making difficult decisions. Avoid overly simplistic decision-making.

- Engage with research more widely, beyond the front page of the EEF's Teaching and Learning toolkit, which provides guidance on average gains and 'best bets' from meta-analysis. There are no guarantees, but the chances of impact improve by fully understanding research and the 'active ingredients' of effective implementation.

- Structural changes that do not lead to better relations between teachers and pupils have limited impact. Smaller class sizes will have limited impact for a high cost if they do not result in better planning for pupil need, more targeted feedback, opportunities for collaborative learning. Are the expectations clear for teachers?

- Are school strategies based on a deep, evidence-based understanding of their school community, or are they based on assumptions?

8. A destination measure

- Are low prior attainers expected to achieve as well as their peers in end of key stage results?

- A successful education is more than a good progress 8 score. Drop out from Key Stage 5 and university is too high for vulnerable pupils nationally. What is the proportion of vulnerable pupils that go on to successfully complete Key Stage 5?

- What is the proportion that goes on to attend and complete university? What is the proportion that secures high quality employment?

- Avoid myths such as 'vulnerable pupils have low aspiration'. Evidence suggests this may inaccurate. Rather, aspirations tend to be high, but the support networks and understanding of requirements of how to achieve those aspirations tend to be missing. Is the evidence on how to impact on pupil aspirations and expectations understood?

9. A CPD measure

- Is professional development sufficiently targeted at the needs of vulnerable pupils and their gaps in learning?

- Is the professional developed based on evidence, with a clear evaluation framework in place?

- Is professional development compliant with the Professional Standards for CPD?

10. An evaluation measure

- Is the school's process and impact evaluation framework sufficiently robust and precise? Are there sufficiently clear internal quality assurance, frequent milestones and SMART outcomes?

- Does the framework enable school leaders to make the necessary adjustments so that there are 'no surprises' at the end of the academic year? Does the evaluation lead to better practice, avoiding vague or simplistic statements?

Further reflections

Each of these measures needs to be underpinned a strong understanding of growing up as a vulnerable young person in the school community. Avoid assumption. Comments such as 'our parents didn't have a good experience of education so don't engage'. This may be true, however a more evidence-based approach is needed to build a strategy upon. This should include professional development for teachers and support staff in meeting the needs of the most vulnerable.

*I have used the term 'vulnerable' to encapsulate pupils who may be disadvantaged, have SEND or additional needs that do not have a formal 'label'. School leaders are best placed to judge who those students are.

This article draws on work as part of the Swindon Challenge.

'If football has taught me anything, it is that you can overcome anything if, and only if, you love something enough.' – Lionel Messi

CHAPTER 17
Talk to the Professionals – Using football to support positive mental health

Manisha Tailor MBE

'I became a carer for my twin brother at the age of 18, who was diagnosed with mental illness as a result of bullying at school. This real life experience, along with my role as a primary school teacher has taught me the value of football and the impact it can have on the mental health of our young people'.

Our mental health and wellbeing impacts upon our everyday lives and is becoming a growing concern for young people. 'Young Minds' suggests that 1 in 10 children have a diagnosable mental health disorder, which is approximately three children in every classroom, and that suicide is the most common cause of death for boys aged between 5-19 years, and the second most common for girls of this age. Mental illness can be caused by a variety of factors such as bullying, bereavement, domestic violence, neglect and emotional, physical or sexual abuse.

Young people need support and intervention to support their mental wellness in a safe and inclusive environment. Research has shown that sport and exercise releases chemicals in your brain that make you feel good – boosting your self-esteem and confidence. I founded the 'Wingate & Finchley FC Disabled Fans Forum' with the support of Fans for Diversity and Freedom for Minds. It is an initiative that allows football fans from within the local area that have a disability – in particular mental health – to come together and enjoy the beautiful game in a safe place, where they can simply be themselves and support their local football club. It is designed to promote an active, healthy and independent lifestyle for adults suffering from mental illness.

This forum allows the adults to get together once a week and develop social skills in a fun environment that they feel comfortable in and one where they are not judged. The integration and acceptance of all is at the heart of this project. Football can play a vital role in empowering those with mental illness to channel their thoughts and feelings into something positive and give them a sense of belonging thus fostering positive mental health.

Through the 'Wingate & Finchley Disabled Fans Forum' we aim to provide:

- A safe environment that fosters confidence, motivation and the feeling of self-worth.
- A variety of football sessions that are fun, fostering engagement, positive participation, teamwork and communication.
- Sessions that promote leading a healthy and active lifestyle.
- Access to Wingate & Finchley FC games where participants and fans can enjoy watching a live fixture and support their local football club.

Participants of the project have commented on friendship as well as the impact it is having on their physical health:

'It was very helpful and important. It helps you with your coordination, to focus, have fun and it keeps you fit. It doesn't make any difference whether you're a boy or a girl, everyone is equal. You can learn from each other'. – Adult participant

'Everyone here is my friend and I come here to meet and play with them.' – Adult participant

A mental health support worker who attends regularly speaks of community engagement, benefits of social interaction and prevention strategies:

'I think it is so important to have projects like this for outside interaction and the wellbeing of these youths. They have the chance to engage with other members of the community, play sports and keep fit – just their general wellbeing. This project prevents those affected by mental health from becoming sedentary or becoming couch potatoes.' – Support worker

Football can be a powerful vehicle for promoting positive mental health in young children and the concept of the 'Wingate & Finchley Disabled Fans Forum' can be replicated in schools.

A practical guide

Empower young leaders:

- The idea of a democratic vote across the school can be used to appoint young leaders to lead on the positive mental health initiative.
- They can decide upon a name that encompasses the notion of inclusion and feeling good
- Create a badge that makes them easy to identify.
- Write a vision statement for the initiative and ensure all members of the school community are aware.

Roles and responsibility of the young people through the initiative:

- Pose a 'Question of the Week' that relates to the subject matter. Children can anonymously write their thoughts on a sticky note and place it next to the question card. This could be discussed during circle time.

- Run a weekly sport session, either lunchtime or after school, that focuses on social interaction and enjoyment.

- Lead on school assemblies based on different topics around wellness, growth mindset and positive mental health (What makes me happy? Who can I talk to if I feel sad? How do I deal with stress?). Assembly themes can coincide with relevant events in the school calendar (e.g. dealing with stress might be pertinent during SATs or testing).

- At lunchtime, be available to create friendship groups and make all children feel included within games and lunch activity.

- If an area within the school or playground is available, this can be created as a 'safe place' and the young leaders can use this for talk or inside games. A school display can also be created to promote positive mental health.

- Have this as an integral part of the school council who can help to drive the initiative throughout the school.

As educators, we have a responsibility to ensure we support young people and provide an intervention to help them in leading a healthy and positive lifestyle. Statistically, three in four children with a diagnosable mental health condition do not get access to the support that they need. Let's use sport as prevention for social challenges and create a school culture that empowers our young people to talk openly about their mental health.

'When today fails to offer the justification for hope, tomorrow becomes the only grail worth pursuing.' – Arthur Miller, Death of a Salesman

CHAPTER 18
Chalkface Survivors: Cyclothymia

Tom Rogers, Head of History

'Cyclothymia, or cyclothymic disorder, is a mild form of bipolar disorder (manic depression). A person with cyclothymia will have a history of mood swings that range from mild depression to emotional highs. Most people's symptoms are mild enough that they do not seek mental health treatment, so cyclothymia often goes undiagnosed and untreated. However, the mood swings can disrupt your personal and work relationships. If you think you have cyclothymia, it may help to see your GP or seek advice from a mental health resource. Cyclothymia can progress into bipolar disorder and people often don't seek treatment until this late stage.' – NHS, 2017

In October 2010, I travelled down to Cardiff to hear a speech by the then Welsh education secretary Leighton Andrews.

I was sat at a table with a number of my colleagues who had also made the trip. I can't remember a thing that Leighton said in a 45-minute address. What I do remember vividly is spending the whole time fantasising about my own death; this recurring and carefully mastered sequence of events involved my driving to Menai Bridge and hurling myself off. Of course, I wasn't particularly keen on the idea of pain, but the escape offered by death was alluring, the comfort of 'freedom' from the intense feelings I had. 'Feelings' that went beyond 'feeling down' – way beyond. My head and heart felt like a tinderbox constantly wanting to catch ablaze.

A few months after Leighton's speech, I found myself sat in the middle of an empty field in North Wales crying uncontrollably, not being able to stop. A lone dog walker had spotted me lying there and called the police. She was a local villager, so she had told them where I lived. They turned up later that night at my door and asked me if I intended to kill myself. Of course I didn't. Nevertheless, this moment perfectly captured what I went through for nigh on a year, day after day, week after week.

I didn't tell anyone at my school anything but I should have

At that time, I had just been promoted. I had just started teaching sixth form and I was halfway through a master's accredited leadership course. I was also aware of being suspected as slightly crazy if I came forward with these revelations. This wasn't because I didn't trust my colleagues – they were some of the most wonderful I've ever worked for or with – but because of the way society is, especially then.

In a paradox I struggle to understand, my productivity continued to increase, my career continued on an upward trajectory.

It was during this time that I drove myself to the hospital at 3am on a school night to tell them I was feeling desperate and, after a few consultations with a psychiatrist, was diagnosed with cyclothymia or 'bipolar lite', as Stephen Fry calls it. At the time, I linked almost all my feelings to the ending of a relationship, but this was naive. Although this 'bout' was the worst I've experienced, over the subsequent seven years, I've had more short bursts of the same; for hours, days, sometimes months, mixed in with occasional 'highs', where I'm the social equivalent of Will Smith.

In 2010, I tried some drugs that didn't seem to quell it. It would be five years before I went back down the medication route.

Teaching with a mental health problem like mine is interesting. Robin Williams comes to mind: a consummate actor and performer who appeared to be one of the most confident, intelligent, witty and 'together' people in the world when he was performing'. Away from the cameras, he suffered bouts of alcoholism and drug addiction, and eventually took his own life.

A member of my family was a primary school teacher of 35 years. He was much loved by the children in his care. He organised the school choir. He wrote his own music. He was committed to his work to the extent that he would rise at 5am every day to complete the necessary tasks before the day. During all of this, he was drinking heavily. They say mental illness runs in families; I've no doubt my uncle suffered. I've also no doubt he didn't consider himself to have a mental health problem, let alone acknowledge it others. He died in his one-bedroom flat. This is what mental illness is. It isn't feeling a bit down and doing something 'happy' to get over it. This is real, deep, and feels unconquerable in the moment.

What do you do if this is you?

The first thing you must do is open up to a colleague, preferably someone in a leadership position within your school. They can be your advocate. It should be someone you trust, but also someone who you feel has the capability and perhaps even empathy to understand your problem. That's why I think it would be brilliant if all schools had a mental health link in either middle or senior leadership for staff, someone who was perhaps honest in their own vulnerability, perhaps someone who was open about their own struggle.

The problem is: how many senior and middle leaders are honest about their own struggle? Very few. If all else fails, please contact a charity such as Education Support or Samaritans.

I will also soon be publishing a list of teachers on Twitter who are open to being contacted to offer anonymous support in the form of a listening ear with a professional lilt.

Don't be ashamed of what your mind is telling you. If you don't think your school will deal with this well, they might surprise you. You never really know what other people think about mental health or what other people have been through. Last week, I revealed on Twitter that I'd taken a day off because I felt awful. The response was very positive from so many teachers across the spectrum of schools, views and vagaries. The response was also extremely positive from my line manager in school. It showed to me that there are a lot of people out there who want to help, but also many more who feel the same way and who just want someone to talk to, even if it's just once every couple of weeks.

Another reason to do this is for the kids. While all kinds of mental illness afflict the children in our care, we try to appear immune to weakness for the most part. This can sometimes be a good thing – modelling strength and resilience. On the other hand, some honesty with the kids about our own 'mind journeys' surely can't be a bad thing. Allowing them to see that their teachers suffer, too – but manage it and successfully do what they need to do – could be a powerful thing.

I hope more educators, male educators in particular, can follow suit

Note from the author...

(Since the publication of the article in the TES, Tom has developed a list of 'Teachers To Talk To'. The details of which may help you or someone you know...)

It begins by stating... All of these teachers are willing to be contacted NOW. It doesn't have to be a crisis, maybe it's something causing you anxiety. Please get in touch with one of them – all are successful, experienced, current teachers who want to listen, not judge. I recommend them wholeheartedly.

It ends with... If you'd prefer to speak to me first so I can connect you with one of these people – please feel free to contact me – Tom, @rogershistory. Also, if you're a teacher willing to be added here (or I've missed you), please get in touch listing name, age, position, area and Twitter handle.

Wouldn't it be great if all schools had this ethos, in which those struggling could speak to someone in the workplace without fear, without stigma, knowing that people care?

References

NHS (2018): Cyclothymia. Available at: www.nhs.uk/conditions/cyclothymia/ (Accessed 22/11/2017).

'I've missed more than 9000 shots in my career. I've lost almost 300 games. 26 times, I've been trusted to take the game winning shot and missed. I've failed over and over and over again in my life. And that is why I succeed.' – Michael Jordan

CHAPTER 19
Failing and why it is so good

What doesn't kill you makes you stronger

Being human, we need to fail often. For some it is a daily occurrence in their position, e.g. sportspeople aiming for gold, for others it is associated with the amount of risk their job entails. Yet it is without doubt that those most successful in life have failed often on their way to establishing themselves. Thomas Edison is a popular example in which, after being asked 'How did it feel to fail 1,000 times?' stated 'I didn't fail 1,000 times, the light bulb was an invention with 1,000 steps'.

In so many schools I see the most able pupils not being challenged enough. I was asked by Roy Blatchford once whether we made our pupils 'cry intellectually at least once a week', and challenge them we should! To fail and bounce back is an imperative quality. To not reach a goal and yet still be able to contextualise this within the wider life picture even more so.

Parents that insist on the 10+ A* and those who do not challenge enough

There are many families in the UK and beyond that pave the way for their children's successes. For them, academic excellence equals a high functioning and well-paid career which they will equate to a life of success, high status and monetary gain. Generally, and I do stress the generalisation of this, this is true. However, the damage that this can cause, especially within a school system that does not stretch the more academic individuals, can lead to potential mental health issues in later life. Schools with these types of demographics must be aware of the cohorts or individuals that are in this bracket in order to reduce the risk.

I sat in the changing rooms at my gym last month and was approached by a very intelligent and well-spoken man. He asked me, because of my role, for some advice. His nephew was always a high flyer at school. Never got a maths question in lessons wrong, never misbehaved, was a dutiful son and well respected by his peers. During his A Levels he froze and ended up having a panic attack on the morning of his third exam. Instead of three A*s he ended college at 18 with one A, one B and one C.

I asked the gentleman if he knew the reasons behind the panic attack. His response was simple, 'he didn't want to disappoint his parents'. Within our conversation it was quickly established that throughout the years his parents had always pushed the message about the importance of academic excellence but never sat him down and said: 'son, you know what, the grades you get are just stepping stones. When you get inside that door it is your personality, you, that counts. Whatever you achieve we will be proud of you and wherever you go we will always cherish and support the path you lead. The key to happiness in life is not defined by grades – it is defined through the contentment you have in your choices and the love you share with others.'

The poor boy was not even worried about himself – he wanted to go to medical school and was offered a place at a still reputable university. However his parents were putting pressure on him to retake the year to get into a Russell Group university. My advice, for what it was worth, talk to your sister, get them to realise the damage they are doing and support the poor boy emotionally – stop with the expectations and provide him support to accept himself.

As schools we are growing and developing tomorrow's generations – some schools sell the academic successes and build reputations around this, assuming that parents will provide the development of the secure mindset around everything else life has to throw at them. When these children grow and at some point experience failure (whether it be a failed marriage, not getting the job they so desperately wanted, not getting a first class honours... or even the journey pushing themselves to the limit to get one), their lack of resilience or perspective could lead to panic attacks, depression, and anxiety which, if left untreated due to shame of not wanting to admit to anyone else their mindset, could lead to more serious consequences.

There are, in every school, those who push themselves to the limits and strive for the highest grades and accolades. Many are self-motivated and are relentless on themselves in terms of expectation. We often associate this with girls more so, particularly in upper primary and certainly in secondary establishments. Yet we miss the bigger picture. Go forward 15 years and look at the biggest killer in men under 45. Suicide.

CALM (Campaign Against Living Miserably), a charity focusing on men, state: 'It's hard to generalise, but many people who think about taking their own lives:

- Are very sensitive to failure or criticism.
- Feel like they have no friends and are isolated.
- Set themselves targets which are difficult to achieve.
- Find it hard to cope with disappointment.
- Find it difficult to admit to having problems they don't know how to solve.
- Find it hard to tell others how they are feeling.'

In 2015, 75% of all UK suicides were male. We can generalise with this and say that women do tend to talk more and therefore are less likely to get into the situation of attempting this.

The point is – suicide or not – academic outcomes, that schools are so under pressure from attaining and pupils are thriving to achieve, mean very little in later life if we do not equip our pupils with a healthy approach and mindset to themselves and to life.

On the flip-side of this are the risks of having low self-esteem based on their own self-concept. It can also be just as dangerous for those who have a poor self-concept, in which they are constantly comparing themselves to others. Placing your most able pupils next to someone struggling sometimes can have a negative effect – leading to a negative self-image. These pupils find it hard to celebrate achievements, lack confidence and later have less motivation to do their best as they are feeling defeated. This is even harder if parents, and schools, do not engage with individuals to bolster their own self-worth and esteem, this allowing them to believe in themselves.

What is a positive mindset?

- Accepting yourself.
- Forging friendships.
- Appreciating all around you – mindfulness.
- Loving interests and activities.
- Explore your feelings.
- Review, rejuvenate, relax.
- Have perspective on what you can and cannot control.
- Use failure to promote successes.
- Be part of the wider community.

There is a better way of experiencing failure

- Aim for all pupils to get at least 10% incorrect on a daily basis.
- Celebrate more the notion of development after being incorrect.
- Actively teach about positive mindsets – be careful of 'growth mindset' unless you are going to do it properly. Many schools say 'we do growth mindset' only to deem this as assemblies, laminated materials and talks within class. To embrace this is a significant task in itself taking schools years to master.
- Teach failure from a very early age.
- Educate parents around healthy mindset to academics and wider life.
- Philosophy for children – enhance thought processes that different opinions are equal.
- Ensure that all pupils hold onto their own self-worth

We need to talk about Freya

I taught Freya a long time ago, but I remember her as a learner in class as clearly as if it was yesterday. Back then a straight Level 5 pupil (todays 'exceeding' pupil), relatively quiet with a good group of three friends. She was also very able in other curriculum areas such as PE and art along with being articulate. An overall high flyer, she told me that when she was older she wanted to be a vet. I saw no reason as to why not.

So it came as a bit of a shock when she knocked on my door to paint my wife's nails. After a while of small talk, I asked her 'Did you not want to be a vet when you were younger?' Her response... 'I still do'.

She obtained exceptional grades in college, yet when it came to going to university she suffered from panic attacks and could not leave the home. She shared that she did not quite believe in herself and that the thought of failing was just too much to bear. I wanted to shake her – tell her that she could, and would, make a fantastic vet and to fulfil her dream. Instead I asked her something else...

'Are you happy?'

The answer... very much so. She enjoyed developing her business, had a wonderful partner that she was set to marry and was still best friends with another pupil who I taught in the same class. For her happiness was found. However, in order to do this she had to accept her direction in life caused by fear of failure.

This taught me a few things worth sharing

- Academic grades will not equal success and access to the dream job on its own. This is something that schools with more affluent and able intakes are to particularly consider.

- Strength of character and sense of wellbeing is an important factor in life achievement.

- Academic success means very little without good mental health.

- Happiness is not defined through necessarily achieving long-term goals.

- Pupils need to experience failure regularly to develop resilience and mindset around it being okay to fail.

Failure is a key skill for pupils to learn and embrace. To be able to reflect and be mentally robust and articulate around barriers should be a non-negotiable within primary and secondary schools, for pupils to be ready for the wider world and to achieve higher successes. It develops strength in character and is useful in employment. It is also a part-preventative to poor self-esteem and can reduce the likelihood of potential suicide. As such, it is an essential part of a successful school's ethos and curriculum.

References
CALM (2017): Suicide. Available at: www.thecalmzone.net/help/get-help/suicide

'There is a loneliness that can be rocked. Arms crossed, knees drawn up, holding, holding on, this motion, unlike a ship's, smooths and contains the rocker. It's an inside kind – wrapped tight like skin. Then there is the loneliness that roams. No rocking can hold it down. It is alive. On its own. A dry and spreading thing that makes the sound of one's own feet going seem to come from a far-off place.' – Toni Morrison, Beloved

CHAPTER 20
Talk to the Professionals – Attachment styles in schools

Dr Sapphire Weerakone and Dr Zenovia Christoforo

With one in ten children aged 5 to 16 years having a clinically diagnosable mental disorder (Office for National Statistics, 2005; Faulconbridge, Hickey, Jeffs, McConnellogue, Patel, Picciotto & Pote, 2017), the role of a 21st century teacher extends beyond delivering lessons to a class. A child's ability to learn and develop cognitively is significantly influenced by their mental and emotional health (Public Health England, 2014), and teachers are increasingly expected to play a role in monitoring and improving their emotional wellbeing (NICE, 2008; Faulconbridge *et al*, 2017) and resilience (Department for Education and Department of Health, 2015; Faulconbridge *et al*, 2017).

To best support a child a teacher must develop some understanding of their problem, and in doing so, should consider a range of factors (Carr, 2006). This chapter will focus on attachment, which is just one of the aspects of a child's development and emotional wellbeing which might contribute to distress and poor functioning.

Attachment

An attachment is a deep and enduring bond between a caregiver and child (Bowlby, 1969) that begins at birth. Through 'social releasers' such as crying, cuddling, suckling, and later, smiling, the infant drives the adult to protect and nurture them. This ensures the survival of the infant, but is also fundamental in setting their expectations of themselves, others, and the world. Through experiencing the responses of their caregiver, infants begin to form an 'internal working model', a sort of blueprint on which they base their expectations of future relationships (Ainsworth, 1971). For example, 'whenever I cry, my mother comes and makes things better. Therefore, I am worthy of care, and if ever I am distressed, someone will help me.'

If a parent responds sensitively and appropriately to a child's needs most of the time, the child begins to recognise their own state of mind, and to understand how to help themselves. For example, if a child cries because they have nobody to play with, a sensitive parent might comment that they seem lonely, and offer or help the child to identify company. The child will learn that the feeling was loneliness, and that finding someone to play with made them feel better. This ability to reflect upon and understand one's own state is called mentalisation, and is crucial to learning to regulate one's own emotions (Jurist, Fonagy, Target & Gergely, 2014). If a child is not supported to manage their emotional experiences, more complex experiences such as shame may become too much to manage, and children may defend again such experiences with the 'shield of shame'; a pattern of lying, blaming, minimising, or raging (Golding & Hughes, 2012). Mentalisation can also be extended to understanding the minds of others, which helps us to understand why others behave the way they do, and how we and others contribute to interpersonal problems or conflict.

The quality of a parent's responses is paramount in setting a child's expectations of how safe the world is, and their ability to survive adversity. Whilst a child with sensitive parents might develop a secure attachment style in which they expect the world to be a safe place where their needs are met, a child with insensitive parents might develop an insecure attachment style and have little faith that others will step in to help or protect them. As such, their focus may be on survival, with adverse consequences for their academic performance (Bombèr, 2007). To better understand the impact of attachment types we will now consider some case studies.

Secure attachment style

> Deepak is eight years old. He lives with his extended family, which included his grandmother until she sadly died recently. Deepak was close with his grandmother and is understandably very sad to have lost her. He is part of a loving, sensitive family where older relatives have made time to talk about what has happened, share memories, and comfort him when he is distressed. Deepak has struggled to concentrate at school this week but has been able to tell his friends and teachers that this is because he is sad and misses his grandmother.

Deepak has a secure attachment style. His family are sensitive to his needs, help him understand his feelings, and offer comfort. Because his internal working model tells Deepak he is loved and loveable, and help is available when he needs it, he can manage difficult and upsetting events, copes with change, articulates how he feels and why, and seeks support when he needs it. With time, Deepak will process his loss and start to focus on his work again. A secure attachment is a protective factor, and children with secure attachment types are generally more resilient and have better emotional health (Bowlby, 1969).

Ambivalent/resistant attachment style

> Elsie is 12, and the oldest of five children. She has no contact with her father, and her mother has struggled with depression for most of her life. Elsie often looks after her younger siblings and does most of the housework. At school, she is disruptive, often calling out and complaining of pains and illness. She has worn trainers to school for the past month, resulting in her spending most of her time in internal exclusion. Elsie has a good relationship with Mrs Byrne, a member of SLT, and seeks her out at least twice a day. Mrs Byrne is fond of Elsie and has worked hard to get her back into class, but yesterday she reached the end of her patience and told Elsie to stop making excuses when she complained of a stomach ache. Elsie threw a textbook across the room, swore at Mrs Byrne, and stormed out of the school. Later she returned to school, was very apologetic and appeared distressed by her own behaviour.

Elsie appears to have an ambivalent/resistant attachment style. Children with this style of attachment experience high levels of anxiety and struggle to believe that they will be held in mind. Their fear of being forgotten leads them to strive to gain attention by any means necessary, be that calling out, constantly asking for help, complaining of illness, or volunteering for every job, in order to be close to the teacher. Elsie's experience of her sole caregiver being emotionally unavailable or responding inconsistently to her needs has taught her that she needs to be persistent and to escalate her signals of need if anyone is to help her. Her anxiety results in her ensuring she has the almost-constant attention of an adult, and she has learned that she can get Mrs Byrne's attention and care by calling out or flouting rules about uniform. However, Elsie's demands can become overwhelming, and when Mrs Byrne finally loses her temper, Elsie becomes distressed and responds by angrily rejecting her. Later, when she is calmer, the anxiety returns, full-force, and Elsie seeks reassurance that she has not lost this vital relationship.

To manage Elsie's behaviour and improve her emotional wellbeing, it is important to understand the root of her difficulties as being an anxiety about being forgotten, or help being unavailable when needed. Over time, Elsie will need to learn that she can be held in mind even when someone is not directly attending to her. A first step might be greeting her by name as she enters the class, and later checking with her that she understands the task. Teachers should set boundaries and targets for Elsie, e.g. 'try this by yourself for five minutes, and I'll be back to see how you are doing'. Over time, these intervals can increase. At present, Elsie is getting more attention for not doing what is expected of her, and this contingency should be reversed by rewarding her with praise and attention when she stays in class and focuses on her work. Similarly, if Elsie sees her peers being rewarded with attention for working hard, this might motivate her to do the same.

Wherever possible, staff should try to limit time-out and help Elsie develop a sense of belonging with her peers so she feels less alone and anxious in class and can reduce her demand on teachers. As Elsie is likely to struggle to mentalise, teachers can help by making comments such as: 'I haven't forgotten you Elsie; I'll be over in just a moment', which will enable Elsie to tolerate a greater interval between direct contacts.

Avoidant attachment style

Josh is 15 and studying for his GCSEs. His parents are both professionals with high expectations of him, and can be very critical. He is a quiet member of the class who has always seemed to just get on with his work. Recently, the class took mock exams and Miss Khalid was shocked by Josh's low grade. She has since noticed that he spends most of the lesson drawing in the back of his book or looking out of the window. He has not accepted offers of help, and has sometimes torn pages out of his book rather than handing them in to be marked.

Josh appears to have an avoidant attachment style; a style which often results in the young person's needs going unnoticed due to their quiet, unobtrusive behaviour. This can result in injuries being missed, as well as educational needs being overlooked. Children with avoidant attachment styles have learned that caregivers are unreliable or harmful, and are wary of forming attachments as this leaves them open to being disappointed or rejected. They strive to be independent, both practically and emotionally, and are reluctant to ask for help. As such, their distress is often unresolved and internalised, and an avoidant attachment style is associated with perfectionism and unrelenting standards.

In Josh's case, his experience of being heavily criticised by parents who expect more than he can deliver has led him to avoid admitting when he is finding something difficult. This in turn has resulted in him underachieving, which perpetuates his need to go unnoticed. As he does not believe others will meet his needs, he rejects help and support, even though this further disadvantages him.

In order to help Josh, it is important to understand his fear of being rejected for being inadequate. He is likely to find it very shaming to have his work openly shared or reviewed and will struggle with group tasks and presentations. Josh might benefit from first learning to be accountable to himself, for example, by privately reflecting on what he has learned, done well, or enjoyed in each piece of work. This will help him to start to see his work as something he is doing for himself rather than for others. He should be encouraged to seek help when needed, using other, less exposing means such as email, when necessary, and supported to build his sense of self-esteem based on things other than academic achievement. Through providing a consistent, encouraging and non-judgemental presence, his teachers can help Josh learn less threatening types of relationships are possible.

Disorganised attachment style

Jade is six. She had a very difficult start to life and is currently in a foster placement. In class, Jade does not listen to the teacher, sometimes going to the carpet to look at a book when she is supposed to be working at her table, snatching pens from other children, and shouting across the class. Sometimes she calls out repeatedly, demanding a change of activity, and at other times she walks out to put her coat on to go out to play far before it is time. At playtime, Jade is bossy and tells the other children what to do. She can be a bully, pushing or biting other children and screaming, kicking, fighting, and punching herself in the head when she is told off.

Jade is showing signs of a disorganised attachment style; a style which results from frightened or frightening care. Early in her life, Jade experienced abuse from her parents. When frightened, her attachment system was activated and she sought comfort from her caregivers, but as they were the source of her fear, she was left with 'fear without solution' (Hesse & Main, 1999). Jade's internal working model is of a scary, dangerous world, where nobody can be trusted and there is no solution to her fear and distress. All of her resources are focused on survival, and she is therefore unable to focus on anything else. Jade tries to control everyone and everything so the world will be more predictable, and lashes out when this doesn't work as she is overwhelmed. Her inability to trust or to regulate her emotions leaves her unable to form relationships or to understand other minds. She is hypervigilant and easily triggered, exploding in response to anything unexpected. As such, school trips and special assemblies intended as or considered a special treat might result in challenging behaviour.

To help Jade, it is important to understand how scared and mistrustful she is. Jade requires consistency and will need a lot of pre-warning and preparation for any change in her usual schedule or routine. Wherever possible, she should be given the option to stay with a familiar person in a familiar place during periods of change. She is likely to benefit from a visual timetable showing her what to expect next, and a consistent member of staff to support her learning and help her stay on task. Jade should be supported to learn to recognise emotions, ideally with the use of pictorial representations, and helped to mentalise for herself and others. She may benefit from a traffic light system whereby she is supported to activate a plan to calm herself down when she feels like her mood is 'amber', with a view to preventing her from reaching 'red' when she loses her temper or melts down. Jade should be helped to notice when her mood is changing, and rewarded for making good use of this system.

Conclusion

Attachment style is just one of many factors that might contribute to a child's emotional wellbeing, but is important to consider in understanding why they behave and relate the way they do. By thinking about the underlying reason for a child's difficulties, we are better able to be compassionate, and to choose interventions that target the underlying distress rather than simply the manifest problems. This in turn, will improve the emotional wellbeing of the child and their ability to learn and relate. Whilst this is not an exhaustive list of interventions, or indeed, presentations, we hope this is a helpful introduction to thinking about attachment styles in schools.

References

Ainsworth, M, Bell, S and Stayton, D. (1971): Individual differences in strange-situation behavior of one-year-olds. In H. R. Schaffer (Ed.) *The origins of human social relations.* London and New York: Academic Press. p. 17-58.

Bombèr, L. (2007): *Inside I'm hurting.* London: Worth.

Bowlby, J. (1969): Attachment and loss. Attachment. New York: Basic Books. Vol 1, no. 2.

Carr, A. (2006): *The Handbook of Child and Adolescent Clinical Psychology: A Contextual Approach* (2nd edition). London: Routledge.

Department for Education and Department of Health. (2015): Promoting the health and wellbeing of looked-after children: statutory guidance for local authorities, clinical commissioning groups and NHS England. London: Department for Education and Department of Health.

Faulconbridge, J., Hickey, J., Jeffs, G., McConnellogue, D., Patel, W., Picciotto, A. and Pote, H. (2017): What good looks like in psychological services for schools and colleges: Primary prevention, early intervention and mental health provision. The British Psychological Society: *Child & Family Clinical Psychology Review*, Vol. 5.

Golding, K. and Hughes, D. (2012): *Creating Loving Attachments. Parenting with PACE to nurture confidence and security in the troubled child.* London: Jessica Kingsley Publishers.

Jurist, E., Fonagy, P., Target, M. and Gergely, G. (2014): *Affect regulation, mentalization, and the development of the self.* New York: Other Press Professional.

Hesse, E. and Main, M. (1999): Second-generation effects of unresolved trauma in non-maltreating parents: Dissociated, frightened, and threatening parental behavior. Taylor and Francis: *Psychoanalytic Enquiry*, Vol. 19, no. 4, p. 481-540.

NICE (2008): Social and emotional wellbeing in primary education. London: National Institute for Health and Care Excellence.

Public Health England (2014): The link between pupil health and wellbeing and attainment. London: Public Health England.

Office for National Statistics, Social and Vital Statistics Division, Office for National Statistics, Health and Care Division, Ford, T. and Goodman, R. (2005): Mental Health of Children and Young People in Great Britain, 2004. UK Data Service.

'If you're going through hell, keep going.' – Winston Churchill

CHAPTER 21
Chalkface Survivors: Teaching with Dissociative Identity Disorder (DID)

Lewis Terry

Having taught in the education sector in various roles for just over a decade, I have come to realise life's success should be measured in terms of happiness. Having self-acceptance, the acceptance of others and a great feeling of self-worth, always put a smile on my face. Attaining this and also having four to five separate personalities was not an easy task, but for now I am here and it is an amazing place to be in.

Mental trauma is hard to understand, especially the rarer the condition. Not much is really understood about DID (Dissociative Identity Disorder), but it is often mistaken for a psychotic disorder and is generally linked to violent sexual abuse as a child. I grew up in a loving nurturing environment, I was never subjected to sexual abuse of any kind and most of all I am not in any way psychotic. Despite the challenges I face, I lead a life as a productive member of society and a positive role model to those around me.

The most useful piece of advice I was told by a teacher was by my secondary school English teacher. She told us that: 'The more creative you are in life, the harder your life will be'. At the time I had no idea how powerful that advice was, or any clue as to what it meant, but ten years later it was and still is the most useful fact I have come across.

As a young child, I was always a little emotionally unbalanced, prone to tears and crying fits for the smallest of things. I was always overly sensitive, causing my teachers to often tire of me, and I spent most of my breaks in detention or alone in the playground with no one to play with. As time moved on, my sister got older, we moved house and I wanted to be stronger within myself, so I began shutting these emotions down. Before I entered my double digits, I was a far more stable child, with a solid friend base and much more successful in my academic work. This was where my routine started. A furious cycle of overworking and never feeling like I had achieved enough. As my outward appearance became more confident and outgoing, my mental state gradually declined.

When I got into my college years my family was going through a difficult time financially due to my dad's poor health. The fear of losing him was very real and it was something none of us knew how to cope with. Over this time, I did a lot of listening and not a lot of talking. I found my friends to be useless at listening and were all wrapped up in the things you consider important when you are 16-17 years old; romance, grades and parties. I didn't have time for any of that as I felt like I was dying. My sleep had declined to three or less hours a night, I was not able to keep down food and I had started hallucinating on a daily basis. It was during this time I first saw my saviour. She was dark-haired, pale and the most beautiful woman I had ever seen. At night I would speak to her, talk through my problems and generally feel at peace. It was evident that this person did not actually exist and that I was also getting beyond sleep deprived, but these encounters were the only thing keeping me from suicide. My thoughts were permanently dark and stepping out of the picture was a very appealing option. I confided in two of my tutors, tried to talk to my family, my doctor and also my friends. No one wanted to know, they said I was being dramatic or were too caught up in their own dramas. A few of my friends at the time said suicide was cowardly and weak. A perspective which I would learn later was common among many people out there. People judge suicide as a horribly selfish act, but unless you have felt that deep inner pain and manic thought process, you can't empathise or understand what is going on in that person's head space. Feel blessed, because when you are in that place there never feels like there is going to be any escaping it.

Thankfully my brain had made me a coping mechanism. It got me through college and into university. In the great expanse of the university campus, a strict routine didn't exist anymore. I was left to socialise at all hours, drink, copulate and knuckle down to work when I needed to. For the first few months I was happy, everything was exciting and fresh. After this initial excitement, my brain started working on overload again. I called home begging to return back to my parents, I wanted a job, regular work but they talked me through it and encouraged me to stick to my plan.

During the next few months I experienced blackouts, I barely slept and was finding it hard to keep track of my life. It was a flatmate at the time that highlighted that I was actually becoming someone else. I was becoming the beautiful young woman from my hallucinations. This news left me hating myself and everyone around me, I became a recluse for a while and incredibly insecure. Switching in and out of my alternate personality left me exhausted and now I knew what was happening I tried to resist it, drinking or taking too much caffeine.

Struggling I went to the campus doctor and confided in him, he accused me of taking drugs and informed me that I was not depressed. Whenever I went back to get help I was turned away, despite never actually taking drugs or causing any problems. I approached my tutors and asked them for guidance but they were not responsive either. One told me that unless I sorted my grammar I would never pass university and perhaps that would be a better focus of my time than looking for meaning in my madness.

As the years progressed I gradually got sicker and sicker. By the second year I was drinking a lot and socialising less. My work output remained but I tended to only go out at night to campus and avoid the daylight. My world had become a nightmarish blend of macabre hallucinations and a sad and meaningless existence. Somehow during this dark point I managed to get a long-term girlfriend, mainly due to the support of my two flatmates at the time. However, by the end of the second year this relationship for many reasons erupted into one awful and horrid night that gained me swift admittance into accident and emergency. My first of many visits. From this moment onward I was put on a suicide watch for two weeks and had nurses come to my room every day and check that I was okay. These were thick set guys, clearly built for restraining people, not making you feel like a human being.

All I had that night was a fit. I screamed, shouted, contorted and collapsed. It was a horrible display, one which thankfully I do not remember but that my friends will never forget. After this point I was seen by a counsellor twice a week, examined by some of the country's leading specialists and put through a wide host of physical and mental testing. All of which came out fine, I was a little low in vitamin D but then what person living in England isn't? I continued to see a counsellor on and off for the next seven years, but I didn't get to see a psychologist regularly until many years after that incident and the many that followed.

My overall attendance at university was almost 100% in the first year, in the second it dropped to 60% and in the last year I attended less than 20%. Due to my drive and my focus, I was able to pass with a 2.2 – 'The Drinker's Degree' as they call it. With the benefit of hindsight, I can say that those years were thankfully the darkest of my life. I was shunned by the medical society, my tutors and was left to guide myself through that darkness. Those that are supposed to guide you onto the right course chose just to look the other way.

My path to teaching was a lot simpler than university. Being given the all clear by multiple medical professionals and told that I did not have to declare my issues with any employers, I went to work as a teaching assistant in a primary school in Redbridge. Having listened to the radio I was well aware that men were needed in primary school so I thought I would give it a try. When I started I was a one-on-one for a registered blind child. It was a fulfilling and enriching experience despite being poorly treated by my class teacher and a few other members of staff because I was male. When it was clear that I had no way to improve my skill set I moved back to my home town to support my family. My mum was having to undergo extensive life adjustments due to a debilitating illness, naturally I wanted to be there to help out. It didn't take me long and I quickly got a job as a one-on-one for a Key Stage 1 girl with behavioural issues. The family stress and adapting to new work and living in a flat on a teaching assistant's wage was hard and mentally I began to go backwards and relapse. My counsellor managed to get me an appointment with a wonderful psychotherapist that swiftly changed my life.

The head at this school didn't want me to become a teacher and had made this very evident, yet due to the support of the deputy head and her belief in me, I was accepted onto the GTP programme in its final year. During this training, I was again made to feel inadequate and useless at my job. One or two lines of positive comment and pages of improvements. It crushed my morale but I had been through worse. I graduated and moved onto another school where I had been accepted for a Key Stage 2 job. On arrival, this turned into a job as a Reception teacher. The work was hard and the days were long. My mentor, who was once outstanding, had been downgraded to requires improvement and the acting headteacher was trying to push her out.

The stress caused me to collapse many times. I caught my head on my sink at home and gave myself a concussion, took two weeks off of work, and then, on my return, quit and vowed never to go back to teaching again. In all of the schools that I had worked they were run by spiteful and hateful individuals that cared little for their staff or children. Teachers were pressured to make up for their leaders' inadequacies and forge and play with data to make the figures look good. Mentally this was toxic for all involved and I decided it was an environment that I no longer wished to work in.

Three months later I returned, after having been self-employed I decided to step into education as a supply teacher in an effort to finish my NQT. The first school I was placed in was the only one I worked in with that agency. It had an awful reputation and the children were without structure or decent staff. I felt at home instantly. The children responded to consistency and a firm but fair approach in teaching. When the academy came in we were given structures and flexibility in the curriculum to focus on social and emotional wellbeing, which allowed the children to flourish. Teaching with the academy was the first time I had felt valued in a career, not just a gutter-runner but a shiny cog in a bigger machine that needed me there in order to run.

Then, towards the end of the first year, I split up with my long-term fiancée and that threw me into a horrible depression and a situation that was very stressful. I passed out a lot, both at home and in school, and I was a liability. It was on this day that I finally discussed the situation of my mental health with my headteacher. To my surprise, I was not thrown out of the door or looked at like a circus exhibit, I was treated like a decent member of staff and he told me to relax and take two weeks off. Later that day the executive head got back in touch with me and had arranged for me to have some assessments done to check I was fit to work in schools. I went along and I was deemed a safe and productive member of society. Like most of these assessments it felt cruel and mentally invasive but it was for the best.

During the therapy that came I found out that I actually had more facets to my personality than I had first thought. This was difficult to come to terms with but with the help of my headteacher, my new girlfriend and a lot of self-analysis I came to terms with it by the end of that year.

Now, almost at the end of my third year at the academy, I feel a sense of belonging. I have been accepted not only by my friends and family but also in my career. All the people that need to know about my mental history and issues are informed and they still respect me for the human being I am. No longer do I feel like a pariah in society, but a strong and productive part of a beautiful institution. I have been allowed to shift from a full-time class teacher into a part-time role that is better suited for me and has some flexibility to it.

Currently I feel very successful in life, I have a great job, a loving partner and a far brighter outlook. Due to this inner peace, I sleep more and have a great deal of control over my multiple personality disorder. There is no good or clean explanation when it comes to dealing with mental health. Over the last decade, my journey has been difficult and spattered with obstacles and greater complications. I hope, in time, that people learn to judge less and listen more. Within the academy I feel like I make a difference and I continue to give the children support every day that I never felt I had from my teachers.

'But I remembered one thing: it wasn't me that started acting deaf; it was people that first started acting like I was too dumb to hear or see or say anything at all.' – Ken Kesey, One Flew Over the Cuckoo's Nest

CHAPTER 22
Best of British Practice

James Kenyon, Chapel End Junior Academy

In order to raise attainment, we believe that enhanced pastoral support and a readiness to learn is key in our pupils' success. To improve the wellbeing, and as a result the academic outcomes, we focus on the following six areas:

- Removing barriers.
- Developing a Pastoral/Inclusion Team.
- Attendance.
- Interventions/Strategies to enable pupil readiness for learning.
- Engaging with key communications within school.
- Empowering parents with the skills to support their children at home.

Removing barriers and developing a pastoral/Inclusion team

Removing barriers	Developing a pastoral/Inclusion team
☐ 360 Approach	☐ Joined up thinking
	☐ Regular scheduled meetings – appropriately shared outcomes
	☐ Pastoral attainment grid***

What is the 360 Approach?

The 360 Approach is designed to enable the pupil to review themselves as learners as well as identify barriers to academic success and wellbeing. The impact of this is reviewed every term for those who are vulnerable and in need of further support.

360 Approach review document

Impact

Autumn: Click here to enter a date.

Spring: Click here to enter a date.

Summer: Click here to enter a date.

360 Review

	Pupil
	Dare of Birth: Click here to enter a date.
	Class: Choose an item.
	Teacher: Choose an item.

Barriers

At Home	In school

Pupil Voice

I find it difficult to ….

You can help me by ….

I can help myself by ….

Strategies to remove barriers

Targets

150

Interventions/strategies to enable pupil readiness for learning and attendance

Interventions/strategies to enable pupil readiness for learning	Attendance
☐ Values system – high priority	☐ Whole school approach/key priority
☐ Breakfast club and positive start to the day/school as a safe space	☐ Bespoke approach/engaging with communities
☐ Intervention for learning and behaviour: learning mentor/play therapist	☐ Tracking monthly/supporting daily for vulnerable children
☐ Behaviour strategies – behaviour policies/ brilliant book**	☐ Monitoring and acting: codes, letters, rewards, motivation, assemblies
☐ Community figures/sports clubs & link to learning	☐ Monthly review

The Brilliant Book**: the power of positivity

The following short interview details the difference positivity can make to pupils showing poor wellbeing or behaviours:

Dad: Child R's case is a bit special. He used to go to a different school and then he moved to Chapel End in the middle of the year. He found it a bit difficult to make friends. The transition did not go very smoothly. I never had any complaints or concerns with the teacher about his education but we had some concern about his behaviour.

Child R: When I was bad I wasn't happy with it. I was sad. Just when I did it and I finished I got angry with myself.

Mr Kenyan: Before the brilliant book was introduced I think he was more noticed for when he wasn't behaving very well. I noticed that it obviously lowers self-esteem so I wanted to do something that would change that and raise his self-esteem.

Dad: Everyone loves to be praised would love to be noticed and have this. And in Child R he is a bit excessive in that. Mr Kenyan introduced the brilliant book. The brilliant book's purpose is to write the good things. Even if the child goes through some problems it won't be written in it so it is only praise. Child R found what he was looking for in a sense of what he loves. He loves to be praised and to be noticed.

Child R: People are now saying good things about me. Not saying 'Oh you're so bad'.

Mr Kenyon: Dad speaks to me regularly. He has noticed that not only is Child R improving at school but at Saturday school, at home.

Dad: Every day when I reach home the first thing is Child R by the door presenting his brilliant book, 'Can you read it Dad – I've got a new comment. New stickers, new cards'.

Mr Kenyon: It installs in the children and in the parents the power of positivity. The power of doing their best.

Dad: We work together the school and at home, the same methodology. He doesn't want to lose this praise. It is not only the brilliant book on its own, but also the brilliant book and the commitment and the continued support we get from Mr Kenyon. I would like to thank him very, very much. His idea is brilliant and he is brilliant.

Brilliant books can be made using a simple scrapbook, writing any positive actions or occurrences during the day. Stickers can be used to accompany these. This is best used when the pupil is also allocated an adult of their choice to meet with the pupil twice a week to look at the book and recognise all of their achievements in school.

Engaging with key communities within school and empowering parents with the skills to support their children at home

Engaging with key communities within school	Empowering parents with the skills to support their children at home
☐ Strengthening governing bodies	☐ Parent workshops
☐ Working with parents: Parent Council/parent volunteers	☐ Language classes
☐ Travelling communities	☐ Online support via the website
☐ Key sports figures	☐ Family Liaison Officer/Welfare Officer/Play Therapist
☐ Social media	

Pastoral support and community engagement are also areas that make a significant difference. So much so, that we audit, together with attendance, our provision and effectiveness. **In order to do this, we action plan and prioritise using the following audit tool. This then forms part of an action plan to ensure that the best care is provided:**

Pastoral assessment grid – this is assessed with two further columns for notes and further actions

Attendance	
Question	**Action**
1. Is there a clear whole school policy?	1a. Check that there is a whole school Attendance Policy in place and that everyone knows their role. 1b. Consider carefully who carries out First Day Response and how effective the practice is. Consider: Who is responsible for ensuring the quality and consistency of First Day Response calls? E.g. are they challenging? The questioning should be rigorous and not too sympathetic where appropriate. Does this person have a formal job title e.g. Attendance Coordinator? After what time are First Day Response calls made? This should be after the time at which registers close. Is the person making the calls able to authorise the absence? How does your office receive the information to carry out the calls?
2. Are staff clear that attendance is a key priority?	2a. Attendance features on the SDP. 2b. Promoting attendance must be everyone's responsibility. Ensure that attendance has a high profile in the school. 2c. Attendance targets are set and monitored during appraisal meetings.
3. Are parents clear that attendance is a key priority?	3a. Induction – explain to parents the importance of attendance from the start, including what good attendance looks like 4% = 7.6 days, 10% = 19 days. 3b. Parents Evening – ensures that all teachers know which parents to discuss attendance concerns with during Parents' Evening.
4. Are children motivated to attend regularly?	4a. Motivate children: assemblies, certificates, badges, class vs. class competitions, mascots, whole school target, letters, etc.
5. Are all children tracked monthly? Are children who are at risk of persistent absence tracked daily?	5a. Establish a clear process for reviewing behaviour concerns monthly and acting upon concerns? 5b. Track every child monthly but track key concerns daily. Ensure that these parents have to phone the HT or DHT to authorise absence.
6. How are the most vulnerable children supported?	6a. Are free breakfast club places available for vulnerable and disadvantaged children?
7. Is contact information up to date?	7a. Half termly information update letters sent out. 7b. Ensure contact details for the most vulnerable are always up to date.
8. Do some families have an 'odd day-off is okay' attitude?	8a. Look for and challenge patterns (long weekends for example) 8b. Meet with parents 8c. Motivate children with individual and class rewards. 8d. Encourage parents to bring children in when a little unwell. They can always be sent home if needed.

9. Do you have travelling families who are away for long periods at a time?	9. Speak with the local authority that they have moved to. Ask whether they can provide a 'dual school' place.
10. Do all parents book appointments after school or after the afternoon register has been taken?	10. Meet with parents to request an after school or after 2pm appointment where possible.
11. Do teachers plan lessons/circle times about attendance?	11a. Ensure that this practice takes place regularly. 11b. Ensure that children understand the importance of attending regularly.
12. Do you have a consistent and well-communicated approach to holiday in term time?	12a. Ensure that your attendance policy makes clear when holidays will definitely not be authorised, e.g. at the start of the school year, during SATs periods. Use your newsletter to remind parents of this at intervals through the year. 12b. Remind parents that ALL members of the class suffer if children take term time holidays as the teacher has to spend time helping some children catch up. 12c. Remind parents also that children miss out on the social side of school life if they take term time holidays, particularly at the start of the new school year.
13. Are you clear about the actions you can take if parents do not respond appropriately to the policy?	Refer to the following guidance: www.gov.uk/school-attendance-absence/legal-action-to-enforce-school-attendance

Pastoral support and readiness to learn	
Question	**Action**
14. Are strategies effective in removing the barriers so pupils are ready to learn?	14a. Choose effective strategies that will remove the barriers for pupils, e.g. social skills groups, free breakfast clubs, learning mentor support. 14b. Monitor the impact of these barriers.
15. Do you carry out team around the school/pastoral meetings to ensure that all support within the school is joined up?	15a. Arrange a meeting each half term that involves all stakeholders for vulnerable children so that all strategies supporting the pupils can be discussed. 15b. Next steps to be identified so impact can be shown in the next meeting.
16. Do pupil progress meetings (PPMs) include pastoral support ideas?	16. Ensure that PPMs always include pastoral support and ensure that these services are offered as a way of increasing pupils performance e.g. play therapy, social skills groups.
17. Is there support for children that do not get support at home e.g. after school homework clubs and extra one-on-one reading?	17a. Include clubs into PP strategy to ensure pupils get support at school they should be receiving at home. 17b. Ensure the clubs offer what 'other' children would offer at home e.g. additional reading, homework.

18. Are your interventions tracked and analysed for impact?	18a. Complete a baseline assessment for the start of the intervention.
	18b. Check progress halfway through the intervention process.
	18c. Complete baseline at the end of the intervention
	18d. Ensure that each intervention is analysed clearly and linked to attainment and progress to show maximum impact.
19. Do you escalate concerns to a preventative service or a learning mentor to ensure that pupils/families are supported?	19a. Have a clear process within school to ensure that any concerns are escalated to the correct service so support can be put in place for the families, e.g. early help.
	19b. Monitor the impact of these.
20. Do you have pupil profile that build a picture of a child from all stakeholders?	20a. Create a file for each class so that all concerns, that are not disclosures, can be collated to build a picture of each child.
	20b. Ensure that the files are checked weekly so that if picture becomes too concerning actions can be sort to support the child.
21. Do you track the impact the pastoral support has on the pupils attainment and progress	21. Set up a tracking document that will combine the impact that the 'menu' support the pupils receive has on the child's attainment and progress.
22. Do you have a strategy where barriers to learning are identified at home and at school?	22a. Meet with parents to identify barriers at home and with teachers to identify barriers at school.
23. Do you have a breakfast club that is free to pupil premium pupils and those that are struggling with punctuality and attendance?	23a. Arrange a free breakfast club or invite pupils to breakfast club so pupils are fed and ready to learn every day.

Parental and community engagement	
Question	**Action**
24. Do you have parent workshops?	24. Set up key workshops linked to school priorities, e.g. phonics in EYFS, Calculation policy so parents can engage with learning of the pupils.
25. Do you engage with particular communities within your school?	25a. Look at key ethnic minority groups – are there key communities that are hard to engage with, e.g. the Gypsy, Traveller and Roma community.
	25b. Liaise with parents from the group and gain trust.
	25c. Invite to become a parent governor to get to know more about the school.
26. Do you have a welfare team/ Family Liaison Officer (FLO)?	26. Appoint a FLO or welfare worker to support with vulnerable families and safeguarding concerns.
27. Do you have open door policy for those families that need immediate support/ talking time?	27a. Ensure that there is someone available that parents and children can speak to on a daily basis.
	27b. Consider this person being somebody other than an SLT member so that parents feel comfortable speaking to them.

28. Have you set up a Parent Council?	28a. Parent council to be set up to represent each class with in the school.
	28b. Half termly meetings to address key issues within the school.
	28c. Provide the parents with actions e.g. choosing whole school values to engage all parents and increase engagement.
29. Do you send past papers home that pupils have already completed?	29a. Send past papers home to parents so that parents can see the question their children have got wrong so that they can support them at home
30. Is your website informative and does it offer interactive support to parents to support children at home?	30. Ensure that website is informative and offers: Interactive videos e.g. calculation policy Clear information about what the child is learning within the class and examples Interactive online links to help pupils at home
31. Have you develop language classes for parent who are EAL?	31. Offer classes to EAL parents so parents can access the learning and support pupils at home.

Through the intrinsic evaluation of these key areas, we can ensure that pupils are provided with high quality care and support. The focus around pastoral and readiness to learn sets the very foundations for positive and effective learning to take place, thus transforming the pathways of many vulnerable individuals.

'I took a deep breath and listened to the old brag of my heart:
I am, I am, I am.' – Sylvia Plath, The Bell Jar

CHAPTER 23

Chalkface Survivors: Depression

Pran Patel

Schools and mental wellbeing

I believe that mental health illnesses are exactly that, illnesses, and should be viewed as such without the fear of stigma and discrimination. As educators it is our social, moral and legal responsibility to create an environment in our classrooms in which pupils and teachers alike feel safe in reaching out for help and support.

Recently, I appeared on BBC London's Inside Out programme with a feature on 'Why Teaching is Making Me Ill'. I disclosed that I, myself, have suffered from bouts of depression, sleeplessness and anxiety. Since the program aired, not only have I been inundated with emails from fellow teachers in solidarity but my pupils have been completely supportive and frank in their questioning. Although I do feel as though I have reduced my employment opportunities in some schools, but do I really want to work those organisations anyway? So all in all a positive experience.

Let me make a point here I refuse to be ashamed of an illness. This is my consistent response to every enquiry which errs on the side of stigma or discrimination, sometimes people brains don't produce enough chemicals for them to function at a 100% all of the time and, I cannot emphasise this enough, that's okay.

Being honest as educators, schools can be pressure cookers for teachers with the inherent stresses of day-to-day issues of working with the volatility of pupils, unachievable numerical exam targets, incessant formal lesson observations, pay related performance management and harsh face of accountability.

Similarly, pupils in their adolescence also have a multitude of stresses if not checked in many cases this becomes a breeding ground for mental health issues for all. As leaders within schools, how do we create a safe environment within the teaching body and as classroom practitioners how do we do the same for the student body?

How school leaders can impact on mental wellbeing

School leaders, senior and middle leaders should be acutely aware of the impact of their actions. When relaying targets teacher self-efficacy has to be in the forefront of their minds, when leaders and follower alike don't believe they can do their task successfully the pressures are often passed down the chain and ultimately to the pupils.

A protective layer of real leadership has to be formed somewhere along the chain as the amount of times I've heard senior leaders make statements such as 'just get the results' and 'you're the middle leader make it happen'. Similarly, I've heard teachers say to pupils 'Grow up you're in Year 11' or 'You haven't started revising. What is the point of me teaching you?'. None of the phrases offers any insight, knowledge or advice to move forward, however it does have the effect of making the pupil or teacher feel pressured and stressed without the tools to solve their dilemma.

School leaders need to recognise honesty and transparency are the structures that form organisation's foundations of culture. Within my current senior leadership team, I feel absolutely no fear of judgement or consequent discrimination as a real trust has been built through long term continuous and honest discourse.

Many teachers and pupils either fear the consequences of reaching out for help or are unaware of the symptoms and illnesses there are going through. Digging into the reasons behind this, often the stigma comes second to the discrimination around mental health. Simply creating a culture where people are not labelled is not enough, fears of discrimination have to put to rest first.

Without the regular conversations trust around our mental wellbeing cannot be built, similarly I would advocate a similar approach with our pupils. Some schools use form tutors/mentors to foster such conversations but I believe this has the most impact if we celebrate the role of teacher in pupil wellbeing. Every teacher is a should be a teacher of mental wellbeing.

Importantly here let me point out that teachers (including myself) are not trained and probably do not have the skills to treat mental illnesses or even identify them. This is okay, accept this and own it; we are not health care professionals. Direct pupils and parents to the right medical professionals.

'Place mask on securely on yourself before you help others'
I would like to make an analogy here; on aeroplanes the oxygen safety mask announcements always end with 'place your mask on securely, before you help others'. If I am saying it's your responsibility to look after your pupil's mental wellbeing, to do this effectively I'm also saying you have to fulfil the same responsibility to your own mental wellbeing.

How do you look check your own mental wellbeing? I live by one steadfast rule, if there is something that has a detrimental impact on your day to day life, that's not okay. Regardless if it is physical or mental in nature, go and seek medical help from your doctors.

Here are my seven tips for the preparation for getting help:

1. Accept that you are not going crazy or mad. The chances are you are ill, accept this, you going for treatment for your illness. Let me say that again, you are at the doctors for treatment.

2. Doctors are often nebulous beings in our lives, they are always there, but do we really know them? Think about and prepare the words to describe how you have been feeling. It took at least two appointments to describe clearly how I was feeling.

3. Get there in good time and think about asking for a longer appointment. I didn't go to my first appointment, I was minutes late and it was easier to cancel than face it. The second appointment wasn't much better, I made a sharp exit mid-appointment when I realised that time was an issue.

4. Be honest with yourself and, consequently, the doctor. You deserve to be happy and don't let anything get in the way of that.

5. Take someone who knows you well with you, that's if you need to, we all get lost for words sometimes or become overwhelmed it's easier to tackle if you have back up.

6. Be open to the doctor's advice, remember they are the professionals. Antidepressants are often regarded as taboo. For some people tablets are the way forward and letting a stigma around a pill stop you from feeling better is silly.

7. Commit to making yourself healthy. This means there may not be a quick fix but a long-term strategy. As practitioners we often commit to our schools and pupils, spending endless hours doing your very best for them. Do the same for yourself you deserve it.

If you are not in a position to support a pupil, do not lament, just use the structures within the school and pass it on to someone who is and recognise you can only give when you are ready and able to give. If you are in a position to support then recycle the above list, use it as script and pass it on. Following this – and this is important whether you supported or passed it on – it is your responsibility to keep checking in with the pupil, parents, teachers and all other stakeholders, mental illnesses do not disappear after a trip to the doctors.

Telling pupils: about yourself or others

The first time I told I pupil that I suffered was around ten years ago. When she felt so alone in the world and thought the feelings of anguish, and anxiety were brought on by her state of mind because she wasn't positive enough and appreciate her life enough.

'It's okay [insert name], I have these sometimes too. Try and breath through it, it'll pass. I know it doesn't feel like it now, but it'll pass.'

As soon as I said it I stuttered, stammered and stopped, was this what I should be telling a pupil during an anxiety attack? Does this make me look weak? Will the senior leadership team find out? Is this the right thing to do? The answers to these questions are yes. Yes, the act of sharing was an act of solidarity, she was no longer alone in the way she felt, it wasn't just her and, more importantly, maybe it wasn't her fault. Yes, it may have made me look weaker as a person of authority by admitting weakness but stronger as a human being, and I'd argue as a real role model. Yes, the senior leadership team undoubtedly found out but surprisingly no issues there either. Yes, I believe it was exactly the right thing to do.

Thankfully from her reaction it was obvious that she needed someone who wasn't afraid of the illness or the stigma. Someone who she could come and talk to when her friends/family thought she was attention seeking. Someone who'd been there when doctor suggested Cognitive Behavioural Therapy and the possibility of medication. Someone to say you're not mad, crazy or nuts you're unwell at the moment and the medical professionals know best.

Being a role model

Whether you like it or not you are a real tangible role model to your pupils. They look up to you. Even on those dreary days when they are all being so annoying they still look up to you, in many cases you are the constant in their lives, not just someone but that someone that, for whatever reason, cares about them.

What does this burden of role-modelhood entail? I'm not going to tell you that teachers must live perfect lives but I do believe as teachers we form pillars on which societies are formed. As role model we should share our adversities and moreover our triumphs over them.

Role models who triumph over adversity are common place in our schools and in wider society, whether it's a triumph through the tribulations of a slum or overcoming a physical ailment for sporting glory. However triumphant roles models with respect to mental health are few and far between, this is mirrored and is a culturally similar to wider society so having them within schools is an absolute must.

Where teachers are fortunate enough to have a robust mental health it's important for them to portrait their understanding and acceptance of the conditions that plague some many others.

We can only hope that the next generation will live up to the values of the role models they see in our schools. Perpetuating through society, changing the world for the better.

'You have brains in your head. You have feet in your shoes. You can steer yourself any direction you choose. You're on your own. And you know what you know. And YOU are the one who'll decide where to go...' – Dr. Seuss, Oh, The Places You'll Go!

CHAPTER 24
The Five Gold Standards

The Five Gold Standards can be used by schools to benchmark and then plan for further improvement in their mental health and wellbeing provision. These standards have been developed by Longwood Primary Academy's WHAM! (Wellbeing, Health, Attendance, Mentality) Outreach team to enable schools to benchmark themselves.

Alternatively, schools can improve self-confidence, resilience and emotional intelligence for pupils and staff by completing the School Mental Health Award developed by the Carnegie Centre of Excellence for Mental Health in Schools (in association with Leeds Beckett University). It details:

'The Department for Education recognises the direct link between positive mental health in schools and successful educational outcomes; the Mental Health Award for Schools builds on this link and provides a framework for educational institutions to evidence policies and initiatives that work towards improving emotional health and wellbeing for both staff and pupils.

The award ensures schools are using evidence-based approaches that align to professional and government guidelines. Utilising a developmental framework, which allows schools to evaluate current mental health practices, identify gaps, develop and strengthen these and work towards building an emotionally healthier environment. Through this process, schools commit to making mental health a strategic priority and developing a positive culture that promotes mental wellbeing for everyone.'

The Five Gold Standards

The Mental Health and Wellbeing Standards for Schools are set out in five Gold Standards:

- Gold Standard 1: Ethos and Values

- Gold Standard 2: Staff Development

- Gold Standard 3: Leadership of Emotional Wellbeing and Mental Health (EWMH)

- Gold Standard 4: School-Based Services and Beyond

- Gold Standard 5: Wider Curriculum and Environment

Gold Standard 1: Ethos and Values

- Positive mental health is promoted by staff and pupils. Pupils are aware of what to do if they feel in need of help and are supportive of those around them.

- A whole school approach to wellbeing for all is owned by all staff and actively promoted, including that of physical health.

- A safe, caring ethos and climate in which relationships and sense of belonging is nurtured and developed.

- Extra-curricular activities are promoted and encourage all pupils with different interests. These provide broad options inspiring all children to work together and to take part.

- Diversity and difference is not only valued and accepted, but celebrated by all.

- The atmosphere of the school (physical and social environment) enables the most vulnerable to feel positive, safe and belonging to the wider school community.

Gold Standard 2: Professional Development and Investment

- Staff, at all levels, are provided with high quality continuous professional development on aspects of wellbeing and mental health according to the school's needs e.g. depression, conduct disorder, child development, factors that impact on mental health, risk taking behaviours, peer mentoring.

- Positive engagement and interactions (relationships) are built, developing high quality communication, participation by all and acceptance in one another's' differences. This is modelled at all levels.

- Staff are provided with time and opportunities to reflect on the wellbeing and mental health of children in their care.

- Resilience in staff is proactively considered, planned for and delivered effectively.

- The school continually reviews the wellbeing, personal health and support mechanisms for pupils and staff – this also includes being able to reflect on staff's own wellbeing and attitudes to mental health. Support is also signposted or provided.

Gold Standard 3: Leadership of Leadership of Emotional Wellbeing and Mental Health (EWMH)

- Mental health and wellbeing is led by a designated person (or collective team) that actively plans and accounts for the quality of provision in the school.

- Safeguarding procedures and training is of highest priority. Staff are well equipped in order to ensure safety for all is of paramount importance.

- Robust identification methods are evident – staff know the warning signs and procedures to ensure that leaders can take action in supporting individuals with EWMH needs.

- Reintegration procedures, following trauma and/or mental health concerns are in place and effective when used.

- The school proactively and effectively signposts the provisions available so that all children know where in the school to find help and what they can access.

- Policies around mental health and wellbeing, including behaviour and anti-bullying are robust and evident in the school's ethos.

Gold Standard 4: School-Based Services and Beyond

- Barriers to learning, and being content, are identified by teachers and other professionals in order to provide individuals with next steps to a secure and fulfilled education.

- The school provides a first-class menu of interventions to address any wellbeing concerns or signs of possible mental health.

- Referrals to outside agencies e.g. EWMHS, doctors are measured and effective in accessing further help for children. Multi-agency support, including the gathering of key information, provides an effective pathway for individuals in need. Partnerships with outside agencies are strong and effective.

- Where a child's needs do not meet external thresholds, the school ensures that excellent support is provided – for example counselling – in order for the individual to succeed within the establishment and, where possible, beyond.

- The school develops and nurtures relationships with parents/ guardians, keeping them fully informed and supporting where necessary in order to access further support.

- The school provides additional support and signposting to the family unit in order for the individual to thrive.

- Within a robust and regular review process, the school identifies clear next steps to success and risk factors that will hinder the development of a child's emotional wellbeing or mental health.

- Transition programmes are effective in ensuring positive experiences for those with anxiety, learning difficulties and apprehension to change.

Gold Standard 5: Wider Curriculum and Environment

- The ethos is reinforced by a curriculum supporting diversity and high quality communication.

- A development of resilience and coping skills intertwines the learning within all subjects.

- The curriculum fosters an understanding in the importance of good mental health, physical health and positive lifestyles.

- All children, and in particular those most vulnerable, are provided with positive, warm and caring guidance and support throughout their learning.

- The school provides children with a place to talk if they are feeling e.g. sad, angry, depressed, resentful, anxious. It is a place where children can 'be' and find sanctuary in their own solitude and/or through positive, supportive relationships from staff or pupils.

- Through an enhanced curriculum and strong ethos, children are involved in developing self-responsibility and an awareness of their duty to and for others.

'There is no greater agony than bearing an untold story inside you.'
– Maya Angelou, I Know Why The Caged Bird Sings

CHAPTER 25
Talk to the Professionals – Establishing a counselling service in school

Kate Armstrong-Taylor

So the case is made as to why schools should invest in promoting, supporting and building the emotional wellbeing of all their pupils, but what about when a more specialist intervention is required?

Thanks to their increased autonomy, schools are in a position to formulate their own strategy for supporting the mental health of their pupils. Appointing an independent counsellor, or indeed an organisation to provide one-to-one therapeutic sessions with children can provide schools with the specialist support some of their pupils need. With the huge variation in provision and associated costs, quality and accessibility to clinical services or appropriately skilled and trained individuals, this could feel like an impossible task. However, having this kind of expertise onsite can have far reaching benefits, not just for the children who are referred for one-to-one work.

Benefits

Early intervention

If a child falls in the playground and grazes their knee, we don't wait for the cut to become infected before we treat it; rather, we clean it up and tend to it in a timely way so the skin can heal quickly with minimal scarring. Why should we not tend to their emotional distress in the same way?

School staff are often able to recognise the signs of emotional distress far in advance of a child developing a serious diagnosable mental illness that might 'meet the threshold' of CAMHS. With a counsellor onsite, this young person can get the early support that could prevent their distress becoming a disorder.

Time

The convenience of a child being able to access counselling onsite is to everyone's benefit: the child can be seen in an already familiar environment; the parents/carers do not have to make lengthy and potentially costly visits to a clinic that may not be near to where they live; time away from learning is minimised as the child does not need to miss school to journey to their appointments.

Referrals

In partnership with the counsellor, schools can influence which referrals should be prioritised and concerns can be shared in the context of what is known about the family situation as well as how the child presents in school. This allows for a joined up approach. Counsellors and teachers can think together, in an ongoing process, about the needs of the child – both therapeutically and in the learning environment.

Leveraging expertise

Once established, the counsellor becomes a recognised and trusted figure around the school. In this way, they can support the wider efforts of the school in the promotion of wellbeing initiatives. Depending on the arrangement entered into with the counsellor, it may be possible to make use of their expertise beyond the therapy room in all kinds of ways: whole class workshops, circle time, running small therapeutic groups and supporting parents as well as teachers. In this way the whole school can benefit.

Space and time

The school will need to give careful thought to the provision of an appropriate space where counselling sessions can take place. It does not need to be large, but it does need to feel safe and secure to those children using it, have a sense of privacy and, ideally, be away from the noise and hectic nature of the classroom.

It should also be made clear to staff that when counselling is in progress, they cannot interrupt nor enter the space.

Liaison

It will be essential to establish a main contact in school for the counsellor as a point of liaison – for the discussion of referrals, arrangement of meetings with parents, other agencies and key staff such as class teachers and safeguarding officers. This key contact would also brief teachers who have children leaving the classroom for counselling, including advising them of the timings of sessions, as well as what the children might need on their return to class, such as support in catching up on missed work or consideration of their emotional state that may mean they need a quiet moment or space before they rejoin the classroom activity.

Confidentiality

Counselling is offered as a confidential service within carefully delineated boundaries. It is important to discuss in advance when, what and how the counsellor will share information with the school. With the exception of safeguarding concerns, schools should not receive lengthy and detailed reports on the one-to-one work.

Options

There are a number of options available to schools seeking to 'buy-in' some sort of therapeutic provision. These range from contracting with an individual or agency, to employing a counsellor directly to buying in a comprehensive service that will embed in the school and can offer a range of interventions to support children, parents and staff. Schools will need to balance an assessment of their needs with the availability of funds to establish the provision with the best fit.

In summary, there are wide ranging benefits to having some therapeutic provision accessible to children in school. There are a variety of options that a school can consider dependant of the level of need amongst the pupils and what the school want from that provision. For any service to be successful, schools need to work closely in partnership with the counsellor. This, in turn, ensures that their expertise can be harnessed in the broadest sense for the benefit of the whole school.

School checklist

- Do make available an appropriate space in which counselling sessions can be held.

- Do assign a main contact to act as a liaison for the counsellor.

- Do hold staff briefings and training around making referrals and the service being proposed.

- Do establish a referral and feedback process with the counsellor.

Counsellor Checklist

- Do they have an appropriate level of training and experience of working with children?

- Have you carried out an enhanced DBS check?

- Do they have an appropriate level of safeguarding training?

- Do they have professional and public liability insurance in place?

- Do they have appropriate clinical supervision in place?

'When people are ready to, they change. They never do it before then, and sometimes they die before they get around to it. You can't make them change if they don't want to, just like when they do want to, you can't stop them.' – Andy Warhol

CHAPTER 26
Charlie and Ronnie

It was pouring with rain, and as I came into the building I was met with a pair of eyes. These I knew only too well. They were the same pair that looked at me before Charlie climbed over the school gate, the same that eyed me closely whilst trying to pick up the netball post and swinging it near my head, and the same that peered into my soul whilst throwing an array of items before going all out and attacking staff. Over time I learnt a few things about this scenario…

1. If I talk to him he will tell me to fuck off and then go into 'fight' mode. After the good punch in the face last week I was not too keen on this.

2. If I walk towards him he will make a run for the fire exit, followed by a quick jump over the fence whilst sticking two fingers up at me.

3. If I walk away he would have won. He also wouldn't have respected it and followed this up with a kick, possibly for attention, partially for entertainment.

I said nothing. I did nothing. I looked away. The meeting in ten minutes with Mrs Bouchard was out the window.

Charlie was standing outside the sports hall. At eight years old, he was the most prolific pupil I had ever come across, including my days in SEND provision. Over the years I have been slapped around the face with excrement, lifted off the ground with hands around my neck, seen a number of staff been sworn at, hit, have their hair pulled, food thrown over them, fire extinguishers set off in their faces. The list goes on, and I am, therefore, at the point in which I am phased by very little. However, this young lad had me trumped for a long time as to the best course of action for him to thrive. The assault on a police officer two weeks before left me with the notion that he cared not for authority of any kind and cared about his life even less.

One of twins, Charlie was the last one standing after this brother, Ronnie, went to a nearby unit for 'alternative provision'. Our concerted efforts before this had led to both attending full-time and having varying successes. However, both being under the same roof seemed nigh impossible, even with full time support and it was decided by all that different placements would be a better option for them to succeed.

The first thing their mum ever said to me was 'I know what you're thinking, they're like the Krays'. I was quite shocked that anyone would say such a thing, although in ways you could not necessarily disagree. Extremely violent and emotionally vulnerable, as a pair they had the potential, and lack of care, to do themselves and others significant harm. Yet, as individuals, they were incredibly charming and you couldn't help but love their character and sense of humour.

The thing that astonished me most was that many saw the two as identical. They looked it. Their behaviours were horrendous – their interests, strengths, even triggers were miles apart. Yet once getting to know them, the two were strikingly different. Their bond with their mother, their inexhaustible energy to break rules and limited care for the effects of their actions was however the same. External agencies were always looking to discharge them, much to our disgust and mum did not want the help from any agency. So, it was down to the school. It was either deal with it or throw them out – the latter not sitting well with my conscience. With Ronnie at another provision Charlie had a chance to cope. We set him up with a significant support package, including someone with him for 31 hours per week whom he had a great bond with and onsite counselling.

He stood there. Fists clenched, head slightly nodding. One step towards him and that would be it. I stayed still.

The reason for all of this, this morning's showdown, was simple. He arrived late into school because he couldn't get his hair right (again) and he was then late for PE, which he hated. Until now he had not entered a PE lesson without cajolement from his one-on-one. She was already in the hall, also not seemingly paying attention in an attempt to see what happened.

Charlie had the ability to do a stand-off for hours – interesting in bad weather and even more interesting if he ever escaped the site. Time meant nothing to him, rules meant very little. It was an interesting situation. 'Should have worn a more comfortable pair of shoes,' I thought, putting my bag down on the floor. I could sense his eyes burning into the side of my head.

After 20 minutes of no eyeballs that could only remind me of a scene in Gorillas in the Mist, I decided to look at Charlie. Eyeballs still. Great! 'Alright?' I asked, nodding my head towards him. Nothing. Not a movement, not a word.

Another five minutes went by. Then his hand raised and held onto the handle of the gym door. Still eyeballs. No other movement. Another two minutes... the door opened. He stood there. I stood there. His one-on-one, on the other side of the door, stood there. I wanted to use praise or acknowledge with some sort of reward on his chart, then resisted as he seemed to be taking ownership of the situation.

'I'm not doing this for you,' he stated calmly, defiantly. 'I'm doing it for her.' He pointed at his one-on-one. And with that, he turned, walked in and took part in PE. I think he did it more for himself, at least I hoped.

That moment, that one step into a room, is still one of the greatest moments I have had in a school. The moment a young boy decided to make a better choice of his own and walk into a room.

I permanently excluded him three months later. As a headteacher I had to get over the feeling that I had failed him and that *our* school was his only chance. I realised that mainstream schools cannot cater for every pupil and that keeping pupils such as Charlie in a limited mainstream setting with limited therapeutic resources would, in fact, result in a less favourable future. It was not easy and took substantial time to admit. With staff I always came back to the question: 'Have we done *everything we possibly can* for this child?'. Until that point the answer was always 'no'.

I still see the family around the locality, our relationship still very positive. The reason for this is because they knew the school did everything they possibly could to support him, including the exclusion for a better chance.

Aspects leading to success with pupils with conduct disorder or similar symptoms

- **Neutral impressions:** This is especially important for those supporting the pupil. Ensure that responses and reactions are as neutral as possible, remaining positive, yet reflective. The development of this and continuity will provide the pupil with a better sense of safety and predictability in care.

- **Deescalation:** Negative expressions can cause escalation in unwanted behaviours. Avoid nagging, shouting, cornering or touching the pupil. Expressions and words that are also negative must not occur.

- **Materials:** At times, due to their behaviour over time, pupils may not be working at age-appropriate levels – ensure that the materials are nevertheless age appropriate – this includes reading books.

- **Non-negotiables:** There are some things that are non-negotiable e.g. harming another, damaging property etc. Do not move from these – they are there for a reason and hold the same consequences for all pupils.

- **Options:** These work well – providing a pupil with two options allows them to feel some control around their actions yet the limited choice helps to provide a constraint around the next step. Avoid direct commands or ultimatums.

- **Clear timetabling:** This allows the pupil to see what is happening during the day and explore possible stress points before they happen.

- **Curriculum:** Ensure the pitch of work is right – if too easy or hard, pupils will switch off and, due to either frustration or boredom, may lead to being disruptive.

- **Praise:** When using praise ensure that it is meaningful and sincere. Do not over use this or make too public.

- **Technology:** Many pupils enjoy the use of technology – if used, ensure that it is meaningful to learning.

- **Rewards:** When developing reward systems ensure that the pupil is also involved in the structure and reward itself. If they have ownership, they are less likely to act against it, rather than on that is introduced or seemingly imposed.

- **Programmes:** Provide access to specific interventions such as conflict resolution or anger management. Lego therapy in small groups and the development of positive social circles can aid turn-taking and socialisation in meaningful contexts.

- **Solidarity with family:** If poor behaviour is displayed or agreements broken, sanctions or consequences are more meaningful when both family and school are aligned in their thinking. This way adults are seen as consistent, this helps in helping the pupil with adult-pupil boundaries.

- **Do not take it personally:** For a majority of the time, their unwanted behaviours are not anything to do with you personally, they are either looking for a reaction or certain outcome.

- **Help the family through signposting:** Many parents of pupils displaying poor behaviour will find this difficult. Signposting and helping parents to access help will in turn aid the school as improvements at home will filtrate into the school environment.

- **Ensure there is a consistent plan:** All staff are to be made aware of who, when, where and how interactions with the pupil should take place.

- **Refer if in doubt:** If the above is being put into place and is having little impact or the initial behaviours are so severe, refer to outside agencies promptly as psychotherapy or behavioural therapy may be needed.

'Life in an autism home is a life lived in a rainbow full of constant chaos, routine, love, laughter, tears, worries, frustrations, celebrations, uncertainties and endless joy… not forgetting lots of wine, chocolate, caffeine, Disney films on loop at 3am, very little sleep, and perfect lines of toys which must not be moved under any circumstances… and woe betide if you run out of that food!' – Autism and other ramblings blog

CHAPTER 27
Chalkface Survivors:
A mother's perspective on ASD and wellbeing

Being a parent of a child with Autistic Spectrum Disorder (ASD) is generally as tough as being a parent to any child – the battles are just different. Before I begin it must be noted, as you probably already know, that no two children with ASD are the same or have the same issues. So the battles presented here are, at times, somewhat individual, however the solutions are beneficial to many.

Being a teacher with a background in SEND, you would think that it would make parenting a child with these difficulties a lot easier. It doesn't, but it does help. Like the fact that we picked up on his speech regression at 18 months so we made an appointment to see a doctor – some wouldn't have necessarily picked it up, or may have gone into denial, or may have placed it down to a result of him being second born. There are other aspects however that no matter your experience, it is still incredibly tough – at times it's embarrassing – at times the best experience that money could never buy.

The day our son's autism was confirmed was a huge shock and very upsetting. Not because of the difference it would make to us as parents, but because of the obstacles that he would face that would his make life so much harder. Facts such as those below make it hard not to worry about whether your little one will lead a happy, independent life:

- Primary school pupils with special educational needs are twice as likely as other children to suffer from persistent bullying.

- 15-year-olds with statements of special educational needs are more likely to be excluded by a group of schoolmates or called names – a form of victimisation that is often referred to as 'relational bullying'.[19]

Or, once they leave school:

- Only 16% of people with autism are in full-time paid work. Only 32% are in some kind of paid work (full and part-time combined), compared to 47% of disabled people and 80% of non-disabled people.[20]

- Over three quarters (77%) who are unemployed say they want to work.

- Four in ten say they've never worked.[21]

So we worry about our children growing up and finding life that can already be difficult, even harder. Park it to the side for now; today matters and it is today that we will make a difference. I know many friends that also have children on the ASD spectrum and this, to some degree, helps.

We all have our own stories, such as:

- The way he enters into birthday parties or goes ice-skating and is completely fearless.

- Reading by sight nearly any given word (much to the annoyance of his older brother).

- Potty training was easy – the more rules and guidance we put in the easier it was. It took only two days.

- The days he ran around on beach for hours in the same patterned course – blissfully happy.

19 Institute of Education. (2014): Are disabled children and young people at higher risk of being bullied? Evidence from two cohort studies of children and young people.

20 Office for National Statistics. (2016): Dataset: A08: Labour market status of disabled people. London: Office for National Statistics. Available at:www.ons.gov.uk/ employmentandlabourmarket/peopleinwork/employmentandemployeetypes/datasets/ labourmarketstatusofdisabledpeoplea08 (Accessed: 20/07/2016).

21 National Autistic Society. (2016): Government must tackle the autism employment gap. Available at: www.autism.org.uk/get-involved/media-centre/news/2016-10-27-employment-gap.aspx (Accessed: 27/10/2016).

- His infectious laughter – never to be taken for granted as so many parents with ASD do not hear their children laugh.

And then there are the other times:

- The high-pitched screaming.
- The scratching and clawing of our faces if he doesn't like something.
- The comments from parents in the playground because he has upset their child in class.
- The fact that if any part of his clothing gets wet they all have to come off – regardless of where we are.
- The branding of some as him being the 'naughty' child – he is not – in comparison, in many ways, quite the opposite.

So like parenting any child there are highs and lows – I could write a similar list for any child I suppose. However, there are certain things that make it that bit harder. When we were told of our son's diagnosis we were handed a leaflet and told to come back in one year, and that was it. We were on our own after a one-day Early Bird parenting class, which to be fair did help. The level of worry and uncertainly is significantly high. Who do parents have to go to? In some communities there are groups for children with ASD, but many are either too far away or some parents are just not ready to take that step. ASD also has a very wide spectrum; for our child who was higher functioning, some groups were not necessarily similar in need. So we have only one other place – our school.

We look to schools for guidance and to provide answers. We have looked on the internet, talked to family and listened to speakers; but the one aspect that makes the biggest difference away from the family unit are the teachers, SENCOs and decisions made by the leadership team that define the five days a week and experience of our child. Before they even start school there is the stress about which one to choose. Are they inclusive? Are they successful with other children with ASD? Are they likely to exclude the second something happens? Are they going to provide our child with the support mechanisms early so that he will thrive? So by the time we start at school we are hopeful, but inside pretty drained, confused and worried.

Then we get to the school – rarely, through discussions with other parents with ASD, has any year gone to plan. There have been surprises, both good and bad, but there were certain things that helped and things that didn't. So, rather than put this in prose, a practical list is below for suggestions from seven parents of children with ASD from different areas in England:

Good ideas	Things that are not so good
• Providing reading books linked to their specific interests to help encourage reading. • Personalised stickers also based on specific interests to acknowledge homework. • A set of toys/items specifically used to reward or calm down a situation quicker for de-escalation or refocusing. • Adapting homework to include their likes and interests. • School trips: Please do think of us first for helping as an additional adult, we can make your life easier too. • Bending the rules with the simple things e.g. allowing squash in their favourite colour cup or bottle instead of just water out of the fountain. • Please share your PECs (Picture Exchange Communication System): We can use the same at home, please do show us how to use these. • Provide courses for parents with disabilities e.g. speech development. If affordable, many would pay for this, knowing it is local and would make a difference. • Leniency for aspects such as uniform so that sensory needs can adjust e.g. school ties not being worn or joggers instead of trousers. • In some cases they may not turn up in uniform, especially in EYFS. If they are dressed as a superhero please bear with us; it took an hour to get out the door. • Increase communication between school and parents: Most are willing to talk before or after school. At times, please realise that we need more of an update than for your average child. • Send a questionnaire to all parents of pupils with ASD. Would they be interested in talking to like-minded parents to discuss their tribulations and ideas? This could lead to support groups and friendships helping us to feel less isolated. • Parenting classes and groups forums for parents to socialise. We often do not get invites to parties due to our child being associated with negative behaviour. • Actively encourage friendships in class. Rotate pupils so that the child gets used to individuals on a one-on-one basis, as groups are sometimes too much.	• Ignorance to disabilities: Please do educate the community around the diversity of the school. • Late diagnoses: Please pick up and act on the early signs. Many report back that the school did not identify ASD until later in school i.e. Year 5. Please do bring in external agencies to see our children if in doubt, especially for classes with new teachers that may not realise the smaller tell-tale signs. • Funding: Many experience that the correct amount of support is not given due to a rejected EHCP application. Provide the support first, and then use this as proof that this is what the child needs in order to gain the additional funding, as time is essential. Our children cannot get the years back. • Speech therapists: These for all of us were limited and some did not have the service. The speech programmes for some are essential to reducing frustration. • SEND departments need to provide clear and regular communication. There was a pattern of parents lacking knowledge of how things were progressing and how things worked – support methods and timetables – within the school and everyday practice. Group meetings (if lacking time) for generic aspects may help.

So there you have it, this is by no means an exhaustive list of what we thought works, and sometimes does not. There are likely to be many aspects for individuals and their schools. At the end of the day, we only really want one thing – for our child to be happy, accepted and to feel loved. Schools have a large part to play in the wellbeing of pupils and their families. We can work together and support one another through the sharing of ideas and approaches.

The next time a parent of a child with ASD walks into the school, looking pretty frazzled, please bear in mind the effort it took to get to the school gates with their child in uniform and with their coat on. It took 45 minutes to put their shoes on and we ran out of rice cakes this morning. Miracles have already happened to get here. A smile and a quick chat can go a long, long way.

'Hello, babies. Welcome to Earth. It's hot in the summer and cold in the winter.
It's round and wet and crowded. At the outside, babies, you've got about a
hundred years here. There's only one rule that I know of, babies–God damn it,
you've got to be kind.' – Kurt Vonnegut, God Bless You, Mr. Rosewater

CHAPTER 28
The End: Ofsted and all that jazz

Ending the book mentioning Ofsted seems somewhat contradictory in terms of the fact that school leaders should do what they feel is right for their pupils first and foremost, regardless of Ofsted. However, when talking to school leaders about our journey, and theirs, the question always comes up: 'But what would Ofsted make of this?'. For some, this question limits their actions or emphasis on wellbeing. Within the larger picture of mental health and wellbeing in our nation being so important, the causal effects in their decisions 20 years from now may affect many lives.

Ofsted

They came and went. Two years and 11 months since opening as an academy, we had the call. For the leadership team there was only one real burning question: 'Are they going to see what we set out to achieve and appreciate the difference it makes?'.

We decided in 2015 that – with such a high proportion of mental health and behavioural needs and low attainment – our efforts should be divided between:

1. High quality teaching and learning.
2. Tackling the mental health and wellbeing agenda.

It was the second that gave us most concern, as it was not necessarily measured as intrinsically as outcomes (only through exclusion rates, behavioural logs and observations in a short window of time). Even back then in 2015, mental health was less prevalent in the media and grossly misunderstood by many professionals and schools. Yet without tackling this agenda proactively the children's academic outcomes would be shallow and surface level.

My deputy and I held onto one voice when in doubt – Sean Harford, who back in June 2015 blogged that: 'the best leaders and practitioners do not ask themselves 'What do I need to do to get a good Ofsted judgement?'. Rather, they should think about what they need to do to **ensure that every child or young person in their school or college gets a decent education and the <u>chance to fulfil their potential</u>.**'

We held onto this for two years. We widened and enriched the curriculum and experiences instead of narrowing them for outcomes gain. We focused more on children as learners and as members of a community rather than drill down on attainment measures. The pressure and stress of doing this and holding firmly to our beliefs took its toll on many occasion for the leadership team, especially due to the multitude of reports of Ofsted being outcomes driven. 80% of our staff had never experienced an inspection and in our Year 6 cohort over 60% were entitled to Pupil Premium.

We stood firm to what we believed was right for our children – the wellbeing agenda to be the most important catalyst in improving holistic and academic outcomes, and that these would improve when coupled with high quality teaching.

The rapid transformation in our children in terms of behaviour, pride and ultimately academic outcomes was due to a very hard-hitting and conscious effort on the team's part to enhance the pupil-teacher relationships, high expectations in everything (in a positive way) and a sense of family within the school. This led to staff wanting to stay and feeling an ownership in the school's direction.

On the second day the inspector turned around and reflected on the behaviour and the way in which the children lined up after play: 'I haven't seen something like that since Sir Michael Wilshaw was a head – very impressive'. We felt very proud of the staff and pupils, yet I was reminded of an article back in 2012 in which Wilshaw was quoted as saying: 'A good head would never be loved by his or her staff.' He added: 'If anyone says to you that staff morale is at an all-time low, you know you are doing something right.'

This made me realise something, as staff morale is currently at an all-time high; there is more than one way to do something and be successful. Whatever you do, you just need to do it well and with good reason. Combine this with what Sean said in 2015 and the message is clear. Do what you feel is best for the pupils and students.

Ofsted did appreciate our methodology and approach to education – to be fair we were given time to talk about the school and our ethos and approaches. We were graded outstanding for Leadership and Management along with (and in our eyes more importantly) Personal Development, Behaviour and Welfare.

All that jazz…

Many schools seemingly feel under the pressure from Ofsted to jump through hoops or ensure that they have certain forms and formats for different aspects of school life. There is still an overriding emphasis on outcomes (mostly due to ASP, IDSR and Ofsted's internal health check system). League tables, progress measures (based on Key Stage 1 data that is four years old) and other aspects data driven such as attendance could still be potentially used divisively in inspections. As a result, there is still an underlying tone that outcomes are the main deciding factor in inspections as it is statistical and as such static evidence.

This is in direct contrast to the wellbeing and mental health agenda in which there are no graphs, progress measures or hard evidence on paper with less emphasis during a visit. The wellbeing of pupils due to the pressure on leaders and teachers for academic outcomes is being potentially placed at a lower status at a time in which it needs to be raised.

Ofsted, as a body, are still currently not necessarily actively helping the wellbeing and mental health agenda as their voice on social media, official documentation and training is still vastly based on outcomes and core subjects. Even the recent publication 'Bold Beginnings' for Early Years Foundation Stage (arguably Ofsted's most debated report of 2017) has a high focus on reading, writing and mathematics and a noted lack on Personal, Social and Emotional Development (PSED) and Communication, Language and Literacy (CLL). Agreed, to get pupils ready for Year 1 in reading, writing and maths is essential; however, further emphasis on the ongoing importance of CLL and PSED would have to be welcomed – particularly in regards to tackling poor wellbeing, communication and mental health. Schools are still ostensibly waiting for

Ofsted to give them the green light to do what they feel is most important; that is to have more emphasis on developing well-rounded pupils over that of grades and results. Yet this is somewhat contradictory when reflecting upon the current education landscape, as 90% of primaries are good or better.

With the ever-changing landscape of schools converting to academies under different trust structures and wellbeing needing to become higher on the school agenda, the following could be recommended as not an end to our current situation, but more of the beginning towards a better mindset.

A few questions linked to wellbeing in schools and inspection processes

- **Should the 'outstanding' grade now be scrapped?** Good or better – with the prose defining the greatness or excellence of a school. With schools being given the Good+ grading, they can feel more free to do what they feel is best (and by that I mean wellbeing) rather than be under pressure to raise to outstanding or sustain this. If good or better is what we as a nation are aiming for, then let them be and not set them to dance a merry tune for something that takes them away from their journey.

- **Was the new move for 2018 in which Section 8 inspections are to be converted within two years to Section 5 for an 'outstanding' grade the best move – is it in the best interests of the children and school staff?** Take a scenario in which a school is at least good – they are then told to expect another inspection (for two days) in the next two years… Staff will be under further underlying pressure (as it could have just been completed the following day under the pre-January 2018 structure).

- **Could safeguarding be inspected by others?** This would allow greater time to focus on the wellbeing and mental health of pupils on inspection, thus adding additional emphasis on this and time to discuss and discover the schools ethos and rationale for being. This also sends a clear message to schools regarding the importance of developing the whole child. In addition, for something as important as safeguarding to be covered within the limited time of an inspection is not the best process for development or auditing. Local Authorities (LA), or independent bodies reporting back to the LA, should spend a day in a school providing a comprehensive annual audit that should be noted by Ofsted when visiting.

- **What would be the harm in increasing the three-year cycle to five or more years?** Say to schools 'we have the data at our fingertips

– if things seem okay then we will leave you alone and see you for one day in five or more years.' Note: children will be safer because safeguarding is audited every year (as mentioned before), the outcomes are telling you a good story – so leave schools alone to do what they do – remembering again that 90% are good or better. Within this use the Regional Schools Commissioners (RSCs) and their teams to sustain 'good' through review visits to those in need of appraisal. This would ultimately let schools do what they feel is best for pupils, setting less emphasis and pressure on outcomes leading to potentially more space to enhance wellbeing and mental health. This in turn would improve outcomes in a more positive way.

- **Should we provide those not 'good' with further support and use public money in a better way to make these good?** The majority of inspectors are now successful leaders in schools. A move towards better Ofsted-School partnerships, trust and cluster models (for peer reviews to take on this role where high quality provision is proven) and adapting in time with the changes in review models would hugely benefit the 10% that are not good. The skills within the inspectorate can lead to those more vulnerable being provided with positive, more regular and highly developmental partners to rapidly improve schools through peer-to-peer support, including that of high quality behaviour and welfare.

- **As a collective (Ofsted together with schools) can we be more mindful of those being home educated?** It took this nation years to get to a point in which all children were given the right to have a decent education by a school. A child is a child is a child. It is their right to a good education and to develop and socialise within a high quality school environment. Yet, their right to this is, at times, taken away by some parents who are not equipped to educate and provide the same facilities. There are currently 30,000 children in England being educated at home. I know this is not necessarily Ofsted's remit, but we could be doing something more about it. There are many vulnerable children whose wellbeing, mental health is underdeveloped, including potential extremism. Ofsted have a powerful voice – this needs to be used more and the high majority of school leaders, I am sure, would back them in challenging government.

For school leaders

- **Look at the current need of your pupils.** If high-achieving, are you ensuring they are challenged so that they are used to experiencing failure within a safe environment? If there are high numbers of those with mental health needs, is your ethos and provision driving part of your school improvement journey? Whatever the context and make-up of your cohorts, the wellbeing and mental health agenda of the school will differ vastly with many schools. One size does not fit all.

- **Place wellbeing and developing the whole child on par with academic outcomes.** I don't for a minute believe that there is any school leader that would not agree, yet so many (particularly those on the back foot on a Requires Improvement or Special Measures grading) are under pressure to increase outcomes when the very thing that would help to increase outcomes is better wellbeing and mental health provision.

- **Staff wellbeing is key to pupil wellbeing.** Better staff wellbeing = higher retention = more continuity for pupils = pupils feeling safer = better learning environments and taking measured risks = better learning = better pupil outcomes = higher self-esteem.

- **Audit the wellbeing and mental health of your school.** Either using the Five Gold Standards or buying into the School Mental Health Award run by the Carnegie Centre of Excellence for Mental Health in Schools with Leeds Beckett University. This will give you the best insight into taking the next step in improving the provision for your school.

- **Have faith in the direction of Ofsted.** Spielman and the team are moving towards focusing more on curriculum, being at the 'heart of educational thinking' and acknowledged in 2018 that this has been wrongly second to performance tables. As such, school leaders have the opportunity to do what they feel is best for their community – academically as well as emotionally. Curricula come in many shapes and forms – know what your values are, develop your curriculum around these, then stand for them.

This book started with 'The reason that people like you or I went into the world of education is to make a difference, and we do.' Yet the difference we make is at times changed by indirect or unintentional external pressures. So I will leave you with the words of Gandhi:

'Carefully watch your thoughts, for they become your words.

Manage and watch your words, for they will become your actions.

Consider and judge your actions, for they will become your habits.

Acknowledge and watch your habits, for they shall become your values.

Understand and embrace your values, for they become your destiny!'

Hold on to what you believe to be right for the children, share it with all stakeholders, make it happen – develop a school whose values hold wellbeing and mental health at the heart of everything you do. When doing so, stand strong for these values and hold onto one thing in particular – kindness. Show it, nurture it and help it to grow in others. If schools do this, everything else that is achieved will hold so much more value to each individual, now and especially later in life when they, and others, need it most.

References

Abrams, F. (2012): Is the new chief inspector of schools just an instrument of government? London: The Guardian. Available at: www.theguardian.com/education/2012/jan/23/chief-inspector-schools-michael-wilshaw (Accessed: 01/12/2017).

Harford, S. (2015): Ofsted mythbusting: dispelling the rumours around inspection – Ofsted: developments in education inspection. Educationinspection. blog.gov.uk. Available at: educationinspection.blog.gov.uk/2015/06/10/ofsted-mythbusting-dispelling-the-rumours-around-inspection/ (Accessed: 01/08/2015).